Asset Protection Handbook

by

Alan F Gonzalez, J.D., LL.M
&
Joseph F. Pippen, Jr., J.D.

Published by
PEARTREE®
P.O. Box 14533
Clearwater, Florida 33766-4533

Printed in the United States of America

Book Order Department
727-586-3306

10 9 8 7 6 5 4 3 2 1

Library of Congress Catalog-in-Publication Data

Gonzalez, Alan F., 1951
Asset protection handbook / by Alan F. Gonzalez, Joseph F. Pippen, Jr.
p. cm
ISBN 0935343-62-8

1.Debtor and creditor—Florida—Popular works. 2. Executions (Law)—Florida—Popular works. 3. Estate planning—Florida—-Popular works. 4. Debtor and creditor—United States-Popular works. 5. Estate planning—United States—Popular works. I. Pippen, Joseph F., 1947 – II. Title.
KFF551.Z9G66 2005
346.75905'2—dc22 2005047663

Disclaimer: This book is intended to answer the most often asked questions concerning legal issues. This book is not intended as a substitute for legal counsel and questions will be answered in general context. Specific legal questions usually have too many variables to give concise, legal answers covering all ramifications. Please consult your own attorney for recent changes in the law.

First Peartree printing, 2005

ABOUT THE AUTHOR

ALAN F. GONZALEZ, J.D., LL.M.

ALAN F. GONZALEZ, attorney-at-law, was born, 1951, in Tampa, Florida. He graduated with a Bachelor of Arts (B.A) degree in Business Administration from University of South Florida, 1973, followed by both a Master of Business Administration degree (M.B.A.) and Doctor of Jurisprudence degree (J.D), from Samford University, 1977. He also obtained a Master of Laws in Taxation degree (LL. M.) from the University of Florida in 1978.

Since being admitted to the Florida Bar, May 31, 1977, his law practice includes the areas of estate planning, asset protection planning, business continuation planning, individual and business tax planning, foreign entity planning and commercial litigation. In addition to his private law practice, he is General Counsel to ACCXX VOIP, LLC, which is an international voice-over-internet (VoIP) telephone systems service provider based in Oldsmar, Florida.

He was admitted to practice law before the U.S. District Court of Appeal for the Middle District of Florida, the Fifth and Eleventh U.S. Circuit Courts of Appeal, the U.S. Tax Court and the U.S. Court of Claims.

He is certified by the Board of Accountancy of the State of Florida as CPA CE sponsor and frequently lectures at CPA Continuing Education seminars on current estate planning, asset protection planning and tax planning topics.

In addition, he was Assistant Professor of Legal Studies at the University of Central Florida, and has also has served as an adjunct instructor at Rollins College, Hillsborough Community, Alabama Christian College and Royalton College.

He is a published author of a civil litigation textbook supplement for paralegal students, along with articles published for insurance industry trade magazines and numerous CPA CE seminars.

He is a noted speaker and lecturer to professional organizations of certified public accountants, physicians, financial planners and attorneys on current tax planning topics.

He is married to his sweetheart, Yolie, and they have three children, Adria, Carly and Kelley. They presently reside in Lutz, Florida.

I dedicate this book to my parents
who mentored me with love

to my beautiful wife
who persevered with me in love

and to the Messiah
who saved me
with His love.

TABLE OF CONTENTS

Asset Protection Handbook

Chapter I
Asset Protection Planning Overview

What is asset protection planning?

Asset protection planning can be defined as the manner in which a person uses various planning techniques so as to protect those assets during his or her lifetime from future potential creditors. Asset protection planning is used as a means to legally protect an individual's wealth. To be sure, asset protection planning does not involve the use of illegal or unethical strategies in order to protect or preserve an individual's assets from future potential creditors. True asset protection planning ***does not*** involve hiding assets from creditors, tax evasion, or defrauding creditors.

Asset protection planning is very much like insurance. You do not buy fire insurance after your house has been destroyed by a fire and you do not buy automobile liability insurance after you have had an automobile accident.

As is true with most things in life, asset protection planning does not guarantee a desired result. Asset protection planning is, in essence, much more of an art than it is a science. Because of this reality, it is critically important that an asset protection plan be formulated and implemented before the client really needs the protection due to creditor claims. A client must obviously implement the desired asset protection plan before he or she needs protection from a creditor's claims, i.e. "buy the insurance policy before a claim occurs".

How does asset protection planning relate to estate planning, tax planning and financial planning?

Asset protection planning is not really a new type of planning. Asset protection planning is directly related to a client's lifetime financial plan, business plan, retirement plan, income tax plan and estate plan. In fact, asset protection planning involves a comprehensive integration of all of a client's planning strategies and is a by-product of the client's operational planning strategies.

Asset protection planning does not occur in a vacuum devoid of other planning considerations. To the contrary, it is critical that any viable asset protection plan achieve desired and objectively meaningful financial, tax, business, retirement planning and estate planning goals. If an asset protection plan only provides for protection of client assets from his or her future potential creditors, then that "asset protection plan" will be vulnerable to attack by creditors and likely to be set aside.

Why do we need to be concerned with asset protection planning?

Due to the fact that we live in a world of legal risk and uncertainty, it is necessary to engage in asset protection planning in order to protect accumulated wealth. Any person in today's society is subject to tremendous financial loss that may result from litigation. It is no secret that we live in a very litigious society with ever expanding theories of tort and contractual liability for everyone regardless of profession, trade or occupation.

Some common areas of legal exposure and risk to the individual are:

1. Environmental law problems at federal and local levels of government, ex. personal liability under *CERCLA*.

2. Divorce.

3. Professional malpractice.

4. Breach of contract, ex. mortgage foreclosure, business failure.

5. Individual liability as a corporate office or director, e.g. breach of fiduciary duty.

6. Landlord liability, ex. slip and fall, mold, defective maintenance.

7. Liability to the Internal Revenue Service, ex. income tax, FICA liabilities.

8. Automobile liability, ex. liability in excess of insurance liability limits, wrongful death.

9. Household liability, ex. dog bite, child drowns in pool at neighbor's home.

10. Business liability, ex. COBRA.

What are the objectives of asset protection planning?

Generally speaking, the objectives or goals of any asset protection plan are as follows:

1. To create an asset protection plan that is understandable and that achieves desired estate planning, tax planning, retirement planning and financial planning goals.

2. The structure of the asset protection plan should protect the client's assets from future potential creditors to the extent legally possible and should be so structured to produce a disincentive for the creditor to pursue the client via litigation.

3. The structure of the plan should create practical and legal bargaining leverage for the client to be able to negotiate a favorable resolution to creditor claims.

4. The structure of the plan should encourage prospective creditors and litigants to settle their claims quickly and at minimum expense.

5. Ultimately, the structure of the plan should be effective, and to the extent legally possible, to preserve the client's assets from seizure by creditors.

What strategies for asset protection are typically used?

Generally, the following strategies are used in any asset protection plan:

1. Block the creditor's access to the client's assets. Some of the various means utilized to accomplish this strategy typically is to incorporate, create a family limited partnership, or limited liability company, to create tenants by the entirety ownership and/or to create an irrevocable trust (which can be either domestic or foreign).

2. Diminish the value of the client's non-exempt estate. The most common method of accomplishing this is to collateralize the assets of the client through the use of a mortgage or security agreement, establish a deferred compensation plan and/or to engage in a sale-lease back of assets transaction.

3. Convert, to the extent possible, all non-exempt assets into exempt assets. *CAVEAT*: *Sec. 222.30, Fla. Stat.* creates the concept of a "fraudulent asset conversion" that limits the use of this strategy. There are a variety of assets which are considered under Florida law to be "exempt" from seizure by creditors, for example:

A. Homestead exemption *(Fla. Const. Art. X, Sec. 4).* There is no dollar value limitation on the Florida homestead exemption. A Florida homestead passes at death of owner to the owner's spouse and children free and clear of creditor's claims (except for certain governmental debts such as IRS tax liens) due to the homestead exemption. The homestead is not devisable to anyone other than the owner's spouse (and then only if there are no minor children surviving the decedent). It has been held that the proceeds of the sale of a homestead with the intent to reinvest the proceeds in another homestead is similarly exempt and protected from creditors. Orange Brevard Plumbing & Heating Co. v. LaCroix, *137 So.2d 201 (Fla. 1962).* There is case law that supports the position that a debtor can convert non-exempt assets into exempt homestead property even if there is an intent to defraud creditors. Havoco of America, Ltd. v. Hill, *2001 WL690070 (Fla. 2001).*

B. Wage exemption *(Sec. 222.11, Fla. Stat.).*

C. Life insurance and annuities *(Secs. 222.13, 222.14, Fla. Stat.).*

D. Pension benefits *(Sec. 221.21, Fla. Stat.).*

4. **Use a special sale arrangement to change asset ownership and replace the asset sold with an asset protected installment sale debt, ex. private annuity.**

5. **Remove assets from Florida to a foreign jurisdiction, i.e. expatriation.** *CAVEAT:* There are negative income tax consequences if motive of expatriation is to avoid U.S. income tax. cf. *Internal Revenue Code ("Code") Sections 877, 6039G.*

What are the asset protection planning tools that are available?

A variety of standard planning techniques that are available in asset protection include:

1. Intervivos gifts.
2. Tenancies by the entireties ownership of property.
3. Statutory exemptions available under Florida law.
4. Family limited partnerships and limited liability companies.
5. Domestic asset protection trusts as authorized in jurisdictions that permit a grantor to retain rights to current trust income such as Delaware, Nevada, Alaska and

Rhode Island. *CAVEAT:* Such a right could be reached by a creditor in a Florida court pursuant to authority of *In re Jane McClean Brown, 303 F. 3d 1261 (11th Cir. 2002).*

6. Foreign trusts and foreign business entities.

How are intervivos gifts used in asset protection planning?

Lifetime gifts can be utilized to dispossess a client of his or her interest in an asset. Lifetime gifts are simple but not necessarily effective in light of Florida's fraudulent transfer statutes as set forth in *Chapter 726, Fla. Stat.*, i.e., "the Fraudulent Transfers Act" ("Act"): This Act applies to any gift that has the purpose or intent to delay, hinder or defraud any creditor. If a lifetime gift falls within the parameters of *Chapter 726, Fla. Stat.*, then that gift may be set aside by a creditor of the donor.

What is the impact of establishing tenants by the entirety ownership of property?

Generally speaking, assets that are owned by husband and wife in the form of tenancy by the entirety cannot be seized by a creditor to satisfy a debt of one of the spouses individually. Recently, there were three separate cases in different jurisdictions that upheld the common law exemption of tenants by the entirety ownership for spouses from creditor attack. *Spears v. Boyd, 308 B.R. 793 (Bankr. W.D. Mich. April 26, 2004), rev. In re Spears, 313 B.R. 212 (W.D. Mich. August 19, 2004) remanded In re Spears, 314 B.R. 360 (Bankr. W.D. September 9, 2004); Musolino v. Sinnreich (In re Musolino) 2004 U.S. App. LEXIS 24693 (11th Cir. 2004); Shlossberg v. Barney, 380 F.3d 174 (4th Cir. 2004).*

Common law dictates that an asset owned as a tenancy by the entirety is immune from seizure by a creditor of just one of the spouses individually. However, if both spouses are jointly obligated to the creditor on a debt, absent any other applicable statutory exemption, that particular asset is subject to seizure by the common creditor of both spouses. Real or personal property is subject to being owned as tenancy by the entireties with rights of survivorship.

Remember that the creation of a tenancy by the entireties does not divest creditors of pre-existing liens that have already attached to the debtor's interest in the property. Also, if a tenancy by the entireties ownership interest has been created to perpetrate a fraud upon a spouse's creditors, then that tenancy by the entireties interest may be avoided or set aside as a fraudulent transfer under *Chapter 726, Fla. Stat.*

What are the statutory exemptions available under Florida Law?

1. HOMESTEAD EXEMPTION: *Article X, Section 4 of the Florida Constitution* provides that the homestead of a natural person is exempt from a forced sale or seizure by a creditor. If a homestead is located outside of a municipality, the extent of the protection is limited to 160 acres of contiguous land along with improvements located thereon. If the homestead is located within a municipality, then the homestead protection is limited to the extent of a one-half (1/2) acre contiguous land. A written statement declaring homestead may be recorded in the public records. *Sec. 222.01, Fla. Stat.*

Personal property is exempted to the extent of value of $1,000.00.

In order to qualify for the homestead exemption, the property must serve as a residence of the owner or his family. The homestead exemption can only apply to the property which is located in the state of Florida. Residence is not a condition precedent to qualifying property for the homestead exemption so long as the property serves as the residence of the client's family or is the owner thereof. The client must have legal title to the property or a beneficial interest in it in order to qualify for the homestead exemption.

There is legal authority standing for the proposition that a debtor can convert non-exempt assets into exempt homestead property, even if the debtor does so with intent to defraud creditors. *Havoco of America, Ltd. v. Hill, 2001 WL 690070 (Fla. 2001); In re Hendricks, 237 B.R. 821 (Bankr. M.D. Fla. 1999); In re Clements, 194 B.R. 923 (Bankr. M.D. Fla. 1996).*

2. WAGE EXEMPTION: *Sec. 222.11, Fla. Stat.*, provides a limited protection from creditor garnishment of wages. Earnings of a person who is "head of family" up to $500.00 per week are exempt from garnishment or attachment while disposable earnings in excess of $500.00 per week may not be attached or garnished unless that person agrees in writing. *Sec. 222.11(2), Fla. Stat.* Disposable earnings of a person who is not head of household may not be garnished in excess of the amount allowed under the *Consumer Protection Act, 15 U.S.C. Sec. 1673.* This exemption shall apply to any wages deposited in any bank account maintained by the debtor when said funds can be traced and properly identified as wages. *Sec. 222.11(3), Fla. Stat.* Commissions earned by an independent contractor are not subject to protection by this exemption. cf. *In re: Moriarity, 27 B.R. 73, (Bankr. 1983).* Alimony is not exempt from garnishment. cf. *Waters v. Albanies, 547 So.2d 194 (1989). See, Sec. 222.11(1)(a), Fla. Stat.*

3. LIFE INSURANCE AND ANNUITIES: *Sec. 222.13(1), Fla. Stat.*, the proceeds of life insurance policies are exempt from the claims of creditors of the insured so long as the insured is a resident of the state of Florida. *Sec. 222.14, Fla. Stat.* further provides that the cash surrender value of life insurance policies and proceeds of annuity contracts issued to citizens or residents of the state of Florida are also exempt from seizure by creditors. This exemption also applies to private annuities. cf. *In re: Mart, 88 B.R. 436, (Bankr. S.D. Fla. 1988). CAVEAT:* Pursuant to the rationale of the *Brown* case, supra, a creditor of a grantor of a trust that pays out a discretionary amount to the grantor of a "self-settled" trust can be reached and that right appears to extend to annuity trusts as well such as CRUTs, as in the *Brown* case, or in GRATs and other similar split-interest trusts.

4. PENSION BENEFITS: *Sec. 222.21(2)(a), Fla. Stat.,* exempts from legal process the qualified plan retirement benefits of any beneficiary or participant. The U.S. Supreme Court has held that ERISA and Internal Revenue Code mandated anti-alienation provisions in a qualified plan causes a debtor/participant's interest in a qualified plant to be excluded from the debtor's bankruptcy estate. *Patterson v. Shumate, 112 S.Ct. 2242 (1992).* IRAs are exempt under the same state statute referenced above.

5. MISCELLANEOUS EXEMPTIONS: In addition to the exemptions already mentioned, Florida law provides for a variety of other exemptions such as:

A. **Unemployment compensation.** *Sec. 222.16, Fla. Stat.*

B. **Disability income benefits.** *Sec. 222.18, Fla. Stat.*

C. **Automobile** (not to exceed $1,000 in value). *Sec. 222.25(1), Fla. Stat.*

D. **Professionally prescribed health aids.** *Sec. 222.25(2), Fla. Stat.*

E. **Prepaid College Trust Fund and Medical Savings Account.** *Sec. 222.22, Fla. Stat.*

How do Family Limited Partnerships and Limited Liability Companies impact asset protection planning?

Lately, family limited partnerships have been actively promoted as a highly effective asset protection planning tool. The basic reason for enthusiasm in using family limited partnerships ("FLPs") as an asset protection tool has been that creditors of limited partners have been generally limited to obtaining a charging order against the debtor/partner as the sole remedy for satisfying the creditor's claim. A charging order gives the creditor the right to receive distributions from the partnership in place of the debtor/partner when and if such distributions are made. A creditor runs the risk when he obtains a charging order that he will be credited with receiving partnership income when there has been no distribution from the partnership. cf. *Rev. Rul. 77-137, 1977-1 C.B. 178.*

Sec. 620.695(a), Fla. Stat., authorizes a Court to impose a charging lien upon a debtor's partnership interest and to appoint a receiver for purposes of receiving that debtor's/partner's share of the profits or other money becoming due to him from the profits or other money becoming due to him/her from the partnership. As always, beware that Florida's fraudulent transfer statute, *Chapter 726*, may be employed to also defeat any asset protection planning use that a family limited partnership may have.

Limited liability companies ("LLCs") are an entity choice alternative that is authorized by *Chapter 608, Fla. Stat.*, and which have attributes of both a corporation and a partnership.

FLPs and LLCs are discussed further below.

Are domestic trusts used in asset protection planning?

Domestically created irrevocable trusts can be used as part of an asset protection planning strategy that may include domestic asset protection trusts ("DAPTs"). DAPTs are authorized by specific state law. There are a variety of different non-DAPT irrevocable trusts (such as grantor retained annuity trusts ("GRATs"), grantor retained unitrusts ("GRUTs") and qualified personal residence trusts ("QPRTs"), that are considered "qualified interest" trusts under *Code Sec. 2702*. These types of trusts have a variety of tax and non-tax estate planning benefits including achieving incidental or limited asset protection objectives.

Typically, non-DAPT trusts involve the making of a completed gift by the grantor. However, the creation of such a domestic trust presumes that the trust was not funded as a result of a fraudulent transfer, that the trust is not illusory and that the grantor who created the trust has not retained too much control of an interest so as to provide a legal basis for recovery by a creditor as against the trust assets. Furthermore, if the Florida-domiciled grantor of a trust "self-settles" the trust, based upon the present application of the *Brown* case, supra, there will likely be no asset protection benefit available for any self-settled trust by a Florida grantor. Apparently, the only possible asset protection benefit available for such a trust scenario would be the protection of the trust corpus of a CRUT or other qualified spilt-interest trust and NOT the protection of the unitrust amount or annuity payable to the grantor/beneficiary annuitant based upon the *Brown* case rationale. Please note that an Alaskan, Delaware or Utah domiciled CRT can now possibly be a protected environment.

A true domestic asset protection trust would have to be formed in a state that has special legislation that obviates the traditional common law "self-settled trust" trap. Since 1997, the states of Utah, Nevada, Alaska, Delaware and Rhode Island have enacted laws that permit a person to create an irrevocable "self-settled" trust that contains a spendthrift provision which, in essence, protects the trust assets and distributions from the trust to the grantor/beneficiary from the grantor's creditors.

In addition to the above-identified states, Oklahoma enacted a statute pursuant to the "Family Wealth Preservation Trust Act" on June 9, 2004, that legalizes the creation of a self-settled asset protection trust ("OKAPT") that can be revoked by a grantor. Under this new and untested statute, there are several unique features: (a) Revocability by the grantor (as mentioned above); (b) Grantor need not be Oklahoma resident; (c) Trustee must be Oklahoma domiciled bank or trust company; (d) Trust assets must be "Oklahoma assets"; (e) Trust must state its income is subject to Oklahoma income tax; (f) Grantor's spouse, lineals and charitable entities are allowable beneficiaries (grantor of the OKAPT is NOT identified as a permissible beneficiary); (g) Only one OKAPT can be created by the grantor at any given point in time, but spouses can create separate OKAPTs; (h) Only $1,000,000 of trust assets are protected (plus incremental trust income retained by the trustee); (i) Trusts can be either revocable or irrevocable. Since these OKAPTs are really new, there are of course a lot of unanswered questions as to the legal benefits of such trusts.

In addition, the states of Alaska, Delaware and Utah specifically provide statutory protection of charitable remainder trust ("CRT") assets from the CRT grantor's creditors and which further protect CRT distributions to the grantor/beneficiary. Since CRTs are self-settled trusts like GRATs, GRUTs and QPRTs, the grantor's interests therein are subject to attack and seizure by the grantor's creditors unless the grantor's interests are otherwise protected by local law. cf. *Lindquist v. Mack, Bankr. D. Minn. 2001; Menotte v. Brown, 11th Cir. 2002; Brown case, supra.*

However, the efficacy of a domestically created "asset protection trust" or DAPT under the laws of those states remains questionable when the grantor is domiciled in Florida due to conflict of laws issues between Florida and the state of trust domicile, different fraudulent transfer laws between the states, and the uncertainty of the application of the Full Faith and Credit Clause and the Supremacy Clause found in the U.S. Constitution.

Many questions abound concerning the actual asset protection effectiveness of DAPTs. Consider the following questions: When there is a Florida grantor of a DAPT created in Delaware, for example, and there is a Florida creditor, which state's law shall apply to determine the creditor's rights against the trust assets? Same example and the grantor files bankruptcy, does federal bankruptcy override state law as to creditor rights? When the state laws of a DAPT's domicile conflict with Florida law, which state's laws shall govern the grantor's rights in the DAPT? Will a Florida court honor another state's conflicting DAPT laws when determining creditor rights against trust assets? These are open questions that create uncertainty in terms of result when using a DAPT. Therefore, because of the judicial uncertainties existing with respect to DAPT law application, utilization of a DAPT should be carefully weighed versus other planning options.

In 2004, the Alaskan legislature passed additional laws that enhance the use of Alaskan DAPTs. These new laws provide protection for QPRTs, GRATs and GRUTs. For Alaskan QPRTs, GRATs and GRUTs, a creditor of the grantor of said trust cannot seize the grantor's right to use the QPRT residence or seize the grantor's retained annuity or unitrust interest in the GRAT or GRUT. An existing trust in another state can be re-domiciled to Alaska if certain conditions are met regarding situs of trust assets, the use of a qualified trustee with requisite powers and place of trust administration.

Are foreign trusts used in asset protection planning?

One possible asset protection tool is a foreign situs trust. A foreign situs trust is a trust governed by the laws of a foreign country. This type of trust has also been referred to as an asset protection trust or an "APT". Typically, the same estate planning and financial planning goals that are sought to be achieved by a domestic trust can also be achieved by the use of a foreign situs trust.

However, there are advantages that a foreign situs trust has over domestic trust has over domestic trust such as:

1. The grantor of a domestic trust is more limited to retain the enjoyment or control of the trust corpus since those trust assets are accessible by the grantor's creditors during the grantor's lifetime to the extent of whatever benefit or control is retained by the grantor. Domestic spendthrift clauses are generally not enforceable with regards to the grantor's interest in the trust corpus. *Sec. 156, Second Restatement of Trusts*, provides that a creditor can reach a grantor's interest in a trust to the extent that he has retained a benefit therefrom. This is the "self-settled trust" problem discussed above and exemplified in the *Brown* case, supra.

2. A domestic trust and its assets is a much higher profile target in litigation against the grantor since the domestic trust is subject to local law. Because of geographical distance and the application of the foreign law of the situs of the trust, a foreign situs trust is not as easy a target as a domestic trust for a creditor.

3. A foreign trust creates a huge practical problem in terms of a creditor attempting to litigate and actually recover assets from a foreign situs trust that will satisfy a judgment. A foreign situs trust increases the practical and procedural complexity of attempting to collect a judgment against trust assets.

4. A foreign situs trust utilizes the trust law of that foreign jurisdiction in which it is created. Typically, a selected foreign jurisdiction will have protective statutes that are more favorable than domestic law would provide.

What recent case law has affected foreign asset protection trust planning?

There have been several cases that have been decided recently in different jurisdictions within the United States that have cast a pall and have generated questions as to how to properly use a foreign asset protection trust. There is no doubt that some promoters and their clients have illegally or unethically used foreign asset protection trusts in order to defraud existing creditors. Obviously, the true purpose of a foreign asset protection trust is only to protect the client from future potential creditors, not existing creditors. A foreign asset protection trust, as a planning strategy, is not rendered invalid due to improper, illegal or unethical use by unscrupulous promoters or clients who intend to protect the fruits of a crime or illegally avoid a creditor's claim. Recently, in the U.S. 9th Circuit Court of Appeals case of *FTC v. Affordable Media, Inc., 179 F.3d 1228 (9th Cir. 1999)*, hereinafter referred to as the "*Anderson case*", the court upheld a lower court's decision to imprison a California married couple on civil contempt charges after the defendants had claimed that is was impossible for them to repatriate certain monies that they had used to fund a Cook Islands asset protection trust. According to the Court records, the Andersons apparently had transferred around $6M of cash into a Cook Islands asset protection trust with all of the cash being derived from an alleged "Ponzi-style" telemarketing scheme. After the FTC discovered the Anderson's Ponzi scheme, it issued an injunction against them and froze their assets and that is when the FTC found out that the Andersons had transferred their cash assets to the Cook Islands asset protection trust. While in litigation with the FTC, the Andersons claimed that they had no control over the Cook Islands trust assets and therefore could not obtain the monies necessary to pay off the FTC claims against them. The court refused to believe that it was impossible for the Andersons to obtain funds from their Cook Islands trust since they had done it previously. It was apparent that the Andersons set up this trust to accomplish the protection of monies earned from a criminal enterprise and it was apparent that the trust was not properly constructed nor administered.

The initial problem was that the Andersons were co-trustees of the trust and were only removed when the threat of a court order forcing them to transfer trust assets caused them to be discharged. The Andersons' trust was also created with the Andersons being protectors of the trust. Again, the fiduciary position as a trust protector gives the Andersons the ability and control over the trust assets to be able to pay the FTC claim.

Due to their fiduciary positions as co-trustees and trust protectors in their own trusts, the Andersons in essence denied themselves the legal ability to claim that it was impossible for them to have access to the trust assets in order to pay the FTC claim. When the Andersons claimed impossibility of performance as a defense to the contempt action, the court merely took the position that the Andersons were not creditable and simply did not believe them. As a result, the Andersons were held in contempt of court for failing to comply with the contempt order which required them to transfer assets from the offshore trust to the FTC in order to settle their claim.

The *Anderson* case provides a case study on how *not* to structure a foreign asset protection trust.

In a recent bankruptcy case, *In re: Portnoy, 201 Bkrptcy. Rptr. 685 (Bkrptcy. DC N.Y. 1996)*, the offshore trust that was created by the bankruptcy debtor was ineffective due to the fact that the debtor had attempted to avoid the claims of existing creditors by creating an offshore trust. Obviously, the foreign asset protection trust is not as effective against existing creditors.

However, the New York State Supreme Court issued a decision in July, 1998, to end the case of *Reichers v. Reichers, 679 N.Y.S. 2d 233 (N.Y. Sup. Ct., 1998)*, that generated a very positive result for the use of a foreign asset protection trust. In that case, which was a divorce case, one of the parties had set up a Cook Islands asset protection trust in order to avoid prospective malpractice liability. Three years later, the spouse filed a divorce action seeking that the trust be set aside and claiming that New York law should apply. The New York State Supreme Court did not agree and held that the trust was set up for valid reasons and not with the intent to avoid any marital claims by the spouse and therefore the foreign asset protection trust was valid and subject to the laws of the Cook Islands as far as determining marital claims.

It is apparent from the above most recent decisions, that in order for a foreign asset protection trust to be effective, the grantor of the trust must not have any past or present creditor claims and the trust must be properly structured. The grantor of a foreign asset protection trust, with the possible exception of a foreign situs grantor retained annuity trust, should never be a co-trustee nor trust protector of that trust.

Beware that the Small Business Jobs Protection Act of 1996 ("Act") enacted tax law changes that impact foreign situs trusts. Prop. Treas. Reg. §301.7701-7 issued June 4, 1997, creates a "court test" and a "control test" that shall determine whether a trust is foreign thus subjecting the taxpayer grantor to foreign trust reporting requirements. IRS Notice 97-34 released June 2, 1997, provides guidance as to the new foreign trust and foreign gift tax reporting provisions required by the above Act.

What about expatriation?

Expatriation is the "final" asset protection strategy. Before considering such an extreme strategy, many personal and tax issues need to be carefully considered with considerable expert advice. Generally speaking, an individual who abandons U.S. citizenship *or* U.S. residency for the principal reason of avoiding U.S. taxes can be taxed on U.S. source income for 10 years following the relinquishment of his or her citizenship or residency unless properly rebutted. *Code Sec. 877; cf. Rev. Proc. 2002-75; IRS Notice 97-19; IRS Notice 98-34.*

Is asset protection planning meant to be a means of illegally hiding assets, defrauding creditors or committing tax evasion?

In no way should asset protection planning ever aid or abet criminal activity of any kind. Asset protection planning should always be incidental to accomplishing primary estate planning and financial planning goals.

Asset protection involves implementing a plan to legally protect wealth.The use of asset protection planning "tools" are subject to *The Uniform Fraudulent Transfer Act* as of January 1, 1988, that was incorporated in *Chapter 726, Fla. Stat.*

Please remember that all of the asset protection tools that have been previously discussed are subject to the purview of the Florida law concerning fraudulent transfers as set forth in *Chapter 726, Fla. Stat.*

What creditors are protected under Florida law from fraudulent conveyances?

Florida's *Fraudulent Transfers Act* is designed to protect two categories of creditors: present and future creditors. Present and future creditors are meant to be protected from debtor transfers made with intent to hinder, delay or defraud such creditors.

The debtor/transferor's intent is a critical factor in determining whether a transaction is considered a "fraudulent transfer". In order to determine such intent, there are certain statutory factors that are enumerated in *Sec. 726.105(2), Fla. Stat.* that must be considered.

1. The transfer or obligation was to an insider.

2. The debtor retained possession or control of the property transferred after the transfer.

3. The transfer or obligation was disclosed or concealed.

4. Before the transfer was made or obligation was incurred, the debtor had been sued or threatened with a suit.

5. The transfer was of substantially all of the debtor's assets.

6. The debtor absconded.

7. The debtor removed or concealed assets.

8. The value of the consideration received by the debtor was reasonably equivalent to the value of the asset transfer or the amount of the obligation incurred.

9. The debtor was insolvent or became insolvent shortly after the transfer was made or the obligation was incurred.

10. The transfer occurred shortly before or shortly after a substantial debt was incurred.

11. The debtor transferred the essential assets of the business to a lien or who transferred the assets to an insider of the debtor.

While present creditors may prove the existence of some or all of the above factors in order to create a presumption of the existence of a fraudulent transfer, a future creditor must show and prove actual fraud on the part of the debtor/transferor.

In more simple terms, a present creditor may be characterized as a creditor of the debtor where the debtor has already committed a tort, breached a contract or breached some other legal duty that is actionable at law. A future creditor may be characterized as a creditor who the debtor intends to defraud. Under Florida's *Fraudulent Transfer Act*, it appears that a future potential creditor is not entitled to protection under the Act. In other words, under *Chapter 726, Fla. Stat.*, not every person who may some day become a creditor of the debtor is entitled to protection under the Act.

What constitutes a fraudulent transfer?

A fraudulent transfer is essentially defined in *Sec. 726.105(1), Fla. Stat.*, wherein it is stated as follows:

1. A transfer made or obligation incurred by a debtor is fraudulent as to a creditor, whether the creditor's claim arose before or after the transfer was made or the obligation was incurred, if the debtor made the transfer or incurred the obligation:

A. With actual intent to hinder, delay or defraud any creditor of the debtor; or

B. Without receiving a reasonable equivalent value in exchange for the transfer or obligation, and the debtor:

(1). was engaged in or was about to engage in a business or transaction for which the remaining assets of the debtor were unreasonably small in relation to the business or transaction; or

(2). intended to incur or believed or reasonably should have believed that he would incur debts beyond his ability to pay as it became due.

Sec. 726.110, Fla. Stat. establishes the time limits for bringing a cause of action under the Act. A creditor who brings an action based upon fraud under this act has within four (4) years after the transfer was made or the obligation was incurred to bring such action, provided, however, that if later, it can be brought within one year after the transfer could have reasonably have been discovered by the creditor.

Where a creditor brings an action for a fraudulent transfer pursuant to *Sec. 726.105(1)(b) or Sec. 726.1606(1), Fla. Stat.*, then the creditor has within four (4) years after the transfer was made or the obligation was incurred within which to bring an action.

Where a creditor's action is based upon a fraudulent preferential transfer to an insider pursuant to *Sec. 726.106(2), Fla. Stat.*, then that creditor has within one (1) year after the transfer was made or the obligation was incurred within which to bring such action.

How do Medicaid eligibility rules impact asset protection planning for a client?

One of the greatest financial risks that a client must face is the possibility of incapacity and the consequential costs of long-term health care. A common fear for an elderly client is the specter of a long-term disability or incapacitating illness that will totally consume his or her assets before death. The question is what planning can be employed that shall guarantee that Medicaid shall pay for the client's long-term health care costs yet not totally lose all assets that have been accumulated during the client's lifetime to the government.

Absent the purchase of long-term disability insurance, which is the most prudent approach to this problem, the client must consider what Medicaid planning strategies make sense and are not going to be illegal or jeopardize Medicaid eligibility. Medicaid planning is quite complex and subject to ever-changing statutory or administrative rules, therefore any client engaging in such planning should employ a qualified legal expert to direct the client's Medicaid planning. The client should be aware the *Kennedy-Kassebaum Act* had criminalized certain transfers involved in Medicaid planning effective January 1, 1997. *42 U.S.C. §1320 A-7(b)(a).*

Remember that Medicaid benefits are designed to assist "eligible" needy persons and which are jointly funded and administered by the federal government and each state. Each state's Medicaid program is unique to that state which makes Medicaid planning complicated and difficult to understand. The federal Medicaid law is found at *42 U.S.C. §§1396, et. seq., and at 42 C.F.R. §§430, et. seq.*

Medicaid recipients who are institutionalized at a hospital or nursing home must use their personal income (less certain allowable items such as personal needs allowance, maintenance needs of spouse, maintenance needs of family, medical care expenses not paid by a third party, SSI or SSP benefits received and home maintenance allowance) to pay for their own care. *42 C.F.R. §435.725(a).*

Any transfer of assets within 36 months of the date of Medicaid qualification by the applicant may cause Medicaid ineligibility. Therefore, asset transfers by a prospective Medicaid applicant for less than fair market value must occur prior to the 36 month "lookback period" in order to avoid Medicaid ineligibility. *42 U.S.C.*

§1396p(c). An exception to the 36 month "lookback" rule exists for the transfer of the Medicaid applicant's home (for less than fair market value) if the transfer of the home is:

1. To the applicant's spouse;

2. To the applicant's child if the child is under 21, blind or disabled;

3. To the applicant's sibling if the sibling owned an equity interest in the house and had resided in the home for at least two years before the applicant's institutionalzation.

4. To the applicant's child if the child lived at the home for at least two years before institutionalization and had cared for the applicant. *42 U.S.C. §1396(c)(2)(A).*

In addition to the above home transfer exceptions to the 36 month lookback rule, the following transfers will not trigger a period of ineligibility:

1. Assets transferred to (or from) applicant's spouse or to (or from) another for the sole benefit of the individual's spouse;

2. Assets transferred to (or to a trust for the benefit of) the applicant's child when such child lived in the house for at least two years before institutionalization and child had provided care to applicant that permitted the applicant to live at home instead of in an institution.

3. Applicant proves to the state that the applicant intended to dispose of assets at fair market value and that the assets were transferred for exclusive purpose other than to qualify for Medicaid or that assets have been returned to applicant.

What Medicaid planning options exist regarding the transfer of assets?

The first and most simple method is to make a completed gift before the 36 month lookback period. Even though simple, this strategy may leave the transferor broke and uncomfortable. This strategy may create negative gift tax and income tax consequences. From an estate planning standpoint, such gifts may be inadvisable. The timing of such gifts are always questionable because no one knows when the needs for institutional care may arise, thus there is no guarantee that the 36 month lookback rule will not be violated.

The client's home can be used as a vehicle to preserve wealth. The home can be transferred to the applicant's spouse. A home could be purchased from non-exempt assets. Existing assets could be used to pay off a home mortgage in order to increase equity in the property. The client's home could be improved structurally.

Beware of utilizing revocable or irrevocable trusts for a prospective Medicaid applicant because special Medicaid rules do apply. The use of trusts in Medicaid planning has been greatly limited since OBRA 1993. There is a 60 month "look-back" period for gifts to irrevocable trusts.

The trust corpus of any revocable trust created by the applicant is counted as resources available to the applicant. Any payments from revocable trusts to the grantor applicant is considered income of the applicant for Medicaid eligibility purposes. *42 U.S.C. §1396p (d)(3)(A).*

In the case of an irrevocable trust created by a prospective Medicaid applicant, Medicaid rules require that if the trust could make payments to or for the applicant's benefit under any circumstances, then the trust corpus and income shall be considered resources available to the applicant. *42 U.S.C. §1396p(d)(3)(B)(i).* There are three types of Medicaid exempt trusts that apply to special trusts for disabled persons. *42 U.S.C. §1396p(d)(4)(A).*

The above rules that are applicable to trusts eliminate the prospect of a Medicaid applicant to create a trust and retain the ability under any circumstances to receive either income or principal from that trust and not have the trust assets count against the applicant for Medicaid eligibility purposes.

In order to qualify for Medicaid benefits that pay for nursing home expenses, the applicant must require that medically necessary level of care.

The State of Florida presently has arguably some of the most favorable laws that protect a Medicaid applicant from losing virtually all of his or her assets due to Medicaid eligibility. In certain circumstances, a Medicaid applicant's estate can be preserved by implementing legally sanctioned planning strategies and still qualify the applicant for Medicaid's Institutional Care Program ("ICP"). It is possible in many instances to avoid the dreaded "Medicaid spend-down" by utilizing "non-countable" asset ownership structures (ex. homestead, one automobile, special annuities, SCINs, some installment notes, household furnishings, burial account not to exceed $2,500, some life insurance contracts, household items and most personal effects, community spouse resource allowance and other allowances permitted by law) for the applicant that take advantage of permissible state exemptions and still allow the applicant to qualify for ICP.

Due to the complexity of applicable state and federal rules for Medicaid eligibility, it is impossible to generalize specific Medicaid eligibility pre-planning or actual planning strategies, however, there some typical planning strategies that may be utilized in the appropriate case that involve the use of the following (the figures used below are for 2005; subsequent years result in different dollar amounts):

Minimum/Maximum monthly maintenance needs allowance ($1,561.25 to $2,377.50). This amount represents a permitted "diversion" of the monthly income of the Medicaid eligible spouse to the other non-applicant spouse, if any.

Community spouse resource allowance ($95,100.00). This protected or exempt amount of assets is available to the other non-applicant spouse, if any.

Resource allowance for individual (the 'asset test") $2,000.00 if only one spouse is applicant and for couple the amount is $3,000.00, if both spouses are applicants, i.e. both spouses are in nursing home.

Income cap amount per month (Institutional Care Program Income) ($1,737.00). This cap is applicable to the applicant only and not to the income of the non-applicant spouse.

Shelter allowance ($468.38). This is available to non-applicant spouse.

Monthly personal needs allowance ($35). This is available to applicant.

$3,300 per month pre-planning gift prior to initiation of receipt of benefits. This is permissible gifting amount that does not disqualify the applicant/donor. All gifts need to be properly reported for gift tax purposes by the donor.

Use of **Qualified Income Trust ("QIT")** to protect eligibility where income exceeds $1,962 per month (the "income test" limitation). The QIT allows applicant to earn more than limit but still maintain eligibility.

Automobile. No limit on value. ***Caveat:*** A sale of auto after qualification can cause disqualification for Medicaid benefits.

Homestead. No limit on value. Same caveat as above in the event of sale of property.

Personal service contract payments.

"Spend-down", allowed pre-payment of expenses or asset purchases e.g. attorney fees (no limit), buy a homestead, repair homestead, buy furniture or personal belongings, pay-off debts, burial savings account, irrevocable funeral or cremation pre-paid contracts (unlimited) and burial expenses ($2,500 limit).

Qualified DCF annuity. *DCAF Manual 165-22, Section 1630.20.10.04.* Only "immediate annuities" may qualify. A Medicaid applicant or community spouse can invest in immediate annuities. The pay-out of such an annuity must equal the life expectancy of the purchaser. An immediate annuity cannot be redeemable during the term thereof. There is no limit on the amount invested in such an annuity.

What ethical problems and criminal liability exposures exist for professionals who give asset protection planning advice?

Inherent in asset protection planning are ethical problems and potential criminal liability.

In the *Florida Rules of Professional Conduct*, it is clear under *Rule 4-1.2(d)* that a lawyer may not counsel a client to engage in or assist a client in conduct that the lawyer knows or reasonably should know is criminal or fraudulent. However, that rule does provide that a lawyer may discuss the legal consequences of any proposed course of conduct with a client and may counsel or assist that client in making a good faith determination as to the validity, scope, meaning or application of the law.

Remember that there is a difference between fraud and a fraudulent conveyance. A fraudulent transfer is a creature of statute, specifically *Chapter 726, Fla. Stat.*, whereas fraud is an intentional tort with specific elements. It is conceivable that an attorney or other professional advisor could be held liable in tort to a third party for participation in a conspiracy that involved a fraudulent transfer. Conceivably, an attorney or an accountant could be deemed to be a fiduciary to a third party and thus have a legal duty to that third party which could be breached.

In addition, an attorney owes certain basic ethical duties to his client:

1. Competent representation, *Rule 4-1.1*.

2. Reasonable diligence, *Rule 4-1.3*.

3. Confidentiality, *Rule 4-1.6*.

4. Absence of a conflict of interest, *Rule 4-1.7*.

Besides the ethical considerations, there are also federal criminal law considerations:

1. In a bankruptcy situation, *11 U.S.C. Sec. 152* provides that: whoever, either individually or as an agent or officer of any person or corporation, in contemplation of a case under *Title 11, U.S.C.*, by or against him or any other person or corporation, or with intent to defeat the provisions of *Title 11*, knowing and fraudulent-

ly transfers or conceals any of his property or the property of such other person or corporation shall be fined not more than $5,000.00 or imprisoned not more than five (5) years or both.

2. *Title 26 of the Crime Control Act of 1990* also known as the *Comprehensive Thrift and Bank Fraud Prosecution and Tax Pay Recovery Act of 1990*, provides criminal penalties for concealment of assets from the conservator, receiver, or liquidating agent of a financial institution.

3. *Sec. 2711* of that same Act provides a criminal penalty for transfers made with the intent to hinder, delay or defraud the creditors specified in the Act.

4. *Sec. 7206(4) of the Internal Revenue Code* provides a criminal penalty for any person that attempts to remove or conceal an asset with intent to evade or defeat the assessment or collection of any tax.

5. *The Money Laundering Control Act of 1986 (18 U.S.C. 1956 and 1957)* was designed to criminally and civilly penalize any person who uses or transfers or otherwise is engaged in a monetary transaction involving funds that are proceeds from specified unlawful activities such as drug trafficking offenses, environmental offenses, financial misconduct, etc.

6. In addition, there is a variety of other federal acts, such as the *Antimony Act of 1992*, that could have an impact on a transaction that involves a person who is deemed to have committed a money laundering offense.

Please note that recently in the case of *Freeman v. First Union Nat. Bank, 865 So. 2d 1272 (Fla. 2004)*, the Florida Supreme Court held that Florida's fraudulent conveyance statute is only a creditor "tool" to be used in order to collect from judgment debtors and not to be used as a legal theory to collect damage claims against non-judgment debtor third parties such as attorneys or financial consultants who have counseled the judgment debtor in attempting to avoid judgment creditor enforcement of said judgment.

Chapter II
FLPs as a Planning Tool

What is a Family Limited Partnership ("FLP")?

A "family limited partnership" (hereinafter referred to as "FLP") is, in reality, merely a limited partnership that is formed under the laws of a particular state whereby the FLP partners are related family members. *§ 620.101- 620.186, Fla.Stat.*, constitute the body of statutory law governing limited partnerships conducting business in the State of Florida and these statutes are cumulatively referred to as the "*Florida Revised Uniform Limited Partnership Act (1986)*".

FLPs are commonly used to produce favorable estate planning, asset protection planning, business continuation planning, transfer tax planning and income tax planning benefits for family members of different generations. The traditional function of FLPs focused on the creation of a business entity, i.e. the FLP, that would effectively manage business and investment assets that are contributed primarily by transferor senior family members to the FLP so as to accomplish tax and non-tax planning objectives such as: (a) redirecting portions of future FLP income to junior family members; (b) creating valuation discounts for transfer tax purposes, i.e. gift tax, of FLP assets for the benefit of junior family members; (c) protecting family assets from future potential creditors of FLP partners; (d) achieving the intra-generational transfers of family assets to junior family members while doing so at a reduced transfer tax cost; and (e) to facilitate business continuation planning for family business assets.

The creation of FLPs involve the creation of management rights and economic rights with respect to the various interests of the partners. In FLPs, there is one class of partners known as the "general partners" and a second class of partners known as the "limited partners". The general partners of a FLP retain both management rights and economic rights over the partnership business. General partners are solely responsible for the management of the partnership business and such general partners are the only partners who have the right to vote on issues concerning FLP management. Limited partners, on the other hand, retain the economic rights as provided for in the partnership agreement, but have no inherent management authority or rights with respect to the operation of the partnership business.

Economic rights include the partner's right to receive allocations of the partnership's distribution of income, losses, deductions and/or credits based upon the agreement of the parties. For purposes of Florida law, see the definitions of "general partner", "limited partner", "partner", "limited partnership", "partnership agreement", and "partnership interest" as set forth in *§ 620.102, Fla.Stat.*

From an income tax standpoint, a partnership generally is not a taxable entity, but is considered to be a "pass- through" entity (unless "C corporation" income tax status is elected by the FLP pursuant to Check-the-Box Regulations; cf. *Reg. § 301.7701-3*) wherein all items of income, gain, loss, deduction and credit are "passed through" to each FLP partner based upon the partnership agreement in each calendar year which is reported by the federal partnership return (Form 1065) filed on behalf of the partnership and as reported in each K-1 that is issued to every partner.

It is essential for income tax purposes that a partnership (including all FLPs) must be bona fide and each partnership transaction must be entered into for a substantial business purpose. All partnership transactions should reflect the substance of what is taking place from a legal and economic perspective (watch out for substance-over-form rules) and the tax consequences of partnership transactions to each partner should accurately reflect each partner's economic agreement and each partner's partnership income in a real way. IRS regulations (known as the "Anti-Abuse Regulations") give the IRS the power to recast transactions that attempt to use the FLP for merely tax avoidance purposes. *Reg. § 1.701-2.*

Furthermore, *Internal Revenue Code ("IRC") §704 (e)* limits FLP business to those business and investment activities that involve capital as a material income producing factor. *cf. Reg. § 1.704-1(e).* FLPs should not be used to engage in business activities that earn income only by the provision of personal services by partners.

In a traditional sense, the typical FLP scenario is as follows. Senior family members, i.e. usually parents, are the primary transferors who set up the FLP and then transfer certain business and investment assets to capitalize the FLP. The FLP agreement is set up so that the parents act as the general partners (or their controlled entity) and the children and/or grandchildren become the limited partner of the FLP. Sometimes the parents retain the limited partnership interest and then make gifts over a period of time of limited partnership units to junior family members. In this scenario, the general partners own a small percentage of the partnership, i.e., usually 1% to 5%, while the limited partners own the majority percentage ownership of the partnership. One of the historical objectives of this type of planning structure is to permit senior family members, as general partners, to retain control of the partnership assets while still transferring significant portions of ownership in the partnership to junior family members.

CAVEAT: Retaining control over FLP income and/or designating who shall enjoy the FLP assets can be considered a "taxable string" to cause inclusion of FLP assets into the estate of the transferor senior family member as per the *Strangi III* case rationale discussed below.

Please beware that as a result of recent case law, most significantly those cases that have been decided concerning the Estate of Strangi (see cites to the *Strangi* line of cases identified below), the structure of the FLP and issues concerning senior family member control of management and of the termination of enjoyment of partnership income must be critically scrutinized and re-evaluated in light of the *Strangi* cases that will be discussed later in this article, to-wit: *Estate of Strangi vs. Commissioner, T.C. Memo 2003-145 ("**Strangi III**"); Estate of Stangi vs. Commissioner, 293 F 3d 279, 89 AFT 2d 2002-2977 (CA-5, 2002) ("**Strangi II**"); Estate of Strangi, 115 TC 478 (2000, aff'd in part and rev'd and remanded in part, 293 F 3d 279, 89 AFTR 2d 2002-2977 (CA-5, 2002) ("**Strangi I**").*

What are the benefits of using a FLP?

Generally speaking, there are a variety of planning benefits available in using and FLP as an appropriate business entity choice:

1. Income Tax Benefits: There are some income tax benefits that are potentially available in using an FLP. By gifting away limited partnership interests to junior family members, partnership income can be legitimately shifted to junior family member who presumably are taxed at a lower marginal income tax rate. Even though income in a limited partnership is typically allocated to percentages of ownership, it is legally permissible to disproportionately allocate income according to business and economic reasons.

2. Preservation of Family Wealth: FLPs can prospectively control distributions of family assets in order to preserve wealth for the benefit of the family.

3. Asset Protection: FLPs offer a degree of asset protection of family assets for partners.

4. Estate Tax Savings: FLPs offer estate tax planning benefits in terms of avoiding probate, providing for a structured plan of management and disposition of family assets and partnership assets may receive the benefit of discount valuations and shift appreciation values to junior generations. CAVEAT: *Strangi III* case rationale discussed herein.

5. Control of Disposition of Family Assets: FLPs can prevent interests in family property from passing to non-family members as a result of divorce, death or other events.

*6. **Effective Gifting Without Fractionalizing Family Asset Ownership:*** FLPs can be used to implement an annual gift giving plan of FLP interests to junior family members from senior family members so as to effectuate transfer tax savings and not fractionalize family asset ownership.

*7. **Effective Asset Management:*** FLPs can avoid minority owners of family assets from being able to impede the management and disposition of such assets.

*8. **Centralized Family Asset Management:*** FLPs provide for central management of family assets.

In spite of the above benefits, FLPs are not for everyone. First of all, as indicated previously, there must be a bona fide and legitimate business purpose for creating the FLP. The days of having a senior family member(s) create and capitalize the FLP with passive assets, retain control of FLP assets and make gifts of minority FLP interests while expecting valuation discounts and excluding FLP asset values from the transferror's gross estate are over!

Recently, there have been a number of FLPs created virtually on the deathbed of a senior family member in an attempt to gain valuation discounts and other FLP planning benefits. This strategy will not work from an Internal Revenue Service ("IRS") estate tax valuation perspective.

FLPs have been created without a bona fide substantial business purpose. FLPs have been created to improperly assign income to junior family members and to effectuate disguised gifts upon creation by senior family members to junior family members. These planning scenarios result in IRS problems since all of these types of scenarios constitute inappropriate uses of the FLP concept. Furthermore, the use of such improper FLP strategies will result in the IRS attacking the structure and seeking tax deficiencies. FLPs are an extremely high risk target for IRS audit. In fact, if you have a taxable estate, you can almost guarantee an audit if one or more FLPs are involved in the decedent's taxable estate.

Thus, FLPs should only be used where appropriate. Competent legal counsel and accounting advice should be sought by the client when structuring any FLP. FLPs are somewhat complex and costly to set up and operate and, as a result, are not appropriate for every estate planning situations. Due to recent case law, it is critical that the documentation for any FLP be carefully drafted so that the FLP design structure complies with all aspects of federal and state law. In order to obtain desired valuation discounts of FLP interests, it will be necessary in light of the *Strangi III* case that senior family FLP partners relinquish sufficient control over management of the FLP assets and over FLP income in order to avoid an *Internal Revenue Code ("IRC" or "Code") § 2036* inclusion problem. This is one consideration of many to be contemplated prior to the implementation of any FLP.

Nevertheless, FLPs remains an attractive planning option for the "right" planning circumstances.

What are the estate planning advantages of using a FLP?

First and foremost, FLPs have been used in an estate planning context in order to obtain valuation discounts of FLP interests by fractionalizing the ownership interests of senior family members in the FLP. Valuation discounts have been obtained for FLP interests for lack of marketability and for minority interests. Due to restrictions on transferability of FLP interests by the partners of the FLP, such restrictions have supported the proposition that such interests are less marketable and therefore entitled to a "valuation" discount.

In general, an asset owned outright that is not owned by an FLP, or other business entity, has a greater value than an entity equity interest in an FLP that owns such an asset directly. The valuation discount for a limited partnership interest due to lack of control and lack of marketability is possible because the limited partner has no managerial control over the FLP assets. By legal definition, the limited partner has no managerial control in the partnership business and cannot force a liquidation of the partnership assets in order to obtain his or her pro rata share of the partnership assets.

There are a variety of factors that are outside the scope of this article that relate to the formulation of valuation discounts of FLP interests. Suffice it to say that such valuation discounts can vary based upon certain factors such as the type of FLP assets owned, the amount of debt financing encumbering the FLP assets, the nature of restrictions on transferability of FLP interests that are provided by state law and/or the FLP agreement, the amount of control by senior family members over FLP assets and income distribution and the manner in which FLP cash distributions are determined by the partnership agreement.

The whole issue of the availability of valuation discounts for FLP interests has been shaken by virtue of the recent and successful IRS attacks on FLPs through the application of *IRC§2036* in cases such as the *Strangi* line of cases referenced above and other cases such as: *Estate of Schauerhamer vs. Commissioner, TC Memo 1997-242, Estate of Reichardt vs. Commissioner, 114 TC 144, 151 (2000), Estate of Harper vs. Commissioner, TC Memo 2002 – 121, Estate of Thompson vs. Commissioner, TC Memo 2002 – 246* and *Kimbell vs. United States, 244 F.Supp. 2d 700 (N.D.Texas 2003).*

In the first five U.S. Tax Court cases referenced above, the Tax Court found that the FLPs reviewed in these particular cases involved an expressed or implied agreement or understanding between the decedent and the other partners of the

FLP that provided that the decedent (who created the FLP in question) would retain effective enjoyment and economic benefit from the property that had been transferred to capitalize the FLP. In these cases, the IRS applied the *IRC §2036(a)(1)* to legally justify finding that the evidence of partnership formation and operation in each case involved an implied agreement or understanding between the decedent and the other FLP partners to create the effect that the decedent retained a *IRC §2036(a)(1)* power of prohibited lifetime control of the FLP assets. In all of these cases the other partners were members of the decedent's family.

In the *Kimbell* case referenced above, the United States District Court found that the FLP partnership agreement was, in essence, an agreement between the decedent and the other FLP partners that permitted the decedent to retain the economic benefits of the property transferred to capitalize the FLP. The Court found that such retained control by the decedent (who initially formed the FLP) caused inclusion of the value of the FLP assets in the decedent's estate pursuant to the authority of *IRC §2036*. However, in a huge defeat for the IRS, on May 20, 2004, the Fifth Circuit Court of Appeals ruled against the IRS position in the case and against the inclusion of FLP assets into the decedent's estate through the application of *IRC § 2036* (see discussion below).

For a long time now, the IRS has been actively attacking FLPs through audits by contesting the percentage of "valuation discounts" applied to the transferred FLP interests. The IRS is now using *IRC § 2036* in order to attack the FLP entity itself in order to eliminate all valuation discounts. The IRS strategy so far has been to attempt to convince the Court that the decedent and/or his or her family members had an implied agreement or understanding that the decedent would retain income or enjoyment of the assets transferred to the FLP until his or her death, thus causing the inclusion of the fair market value of all FLP assets in the decedent's estate due to the application of *IRC § 2036*.

IRC §2036(a) states as follows: *"the value of the gross estate shall include the value of all property to the extent of any interest therein which the decedent has at anytime made a transfer (except in case of a bona fide sale for an adequate and full consideration of money or monies worth), by trust or otherwise, under which he obtained for his life or for any period not ascertainable without reference to his death, or for any period which does not in fact end before his death – (1) the possession or enjoyment of, or the right to the income from, property, or (2) the right, either alone or in conjunction with any persons, to designate the persons who shall possess or enjoy the property or the income therefrom."*

It will be interesting to see if the mode of IRS attack on FLPs shall change in light of the *Kimbell* and *Strangi III* cases, supra.

What is the typical FLP structure and what assets are typically used to fund the FLP?

The typical FLP scenario involves parents creating a FLP and transferring income producing capital assets into the partnership for the ultimate benefit of their children and grandchildren. A transfer of assets to a FLP is not a gift but a capital contribution to the partnership in exchange for which the parents receive general and limited partnership interests. This exchange is considered a tax-free exchange of assets pursuant to *IRC §721(a),* unless the "investment company" exception set for in *IRC §721(b)* applies. Beware that the non-recognition rule of *IRC §721(a)* mentioned above will not apply to any gain realized on a transfer to a partnership which would have been treated as an "investment company" under *IRC §351(e).*

A partnership is an "investment company" for purposes of *IRC §721(b)* if the transfer results in "diversification" and, that after the relevant exchange, more than 80% of the value of the FLP assets transferred are held for investment and consist of "stock and securities" or interest in regulated investment companies or real estate investment trusts. Cf. *Reg. 1.351-1(c)(1);IRC §351(e)(1).*

Subject to avoiding the partnership being classified as an investment company partnership, the FLP can be funded with business, personal or investment assets.

After the FLP is created and funded, the parents or their controlled entities typically become the general partners and, either initially or over time, the limited partnership interests are transferred by gift or sale to the parents' children or grandchildren. The general partners usually retain only a small portion of the ownership of the limited partnership while the limited partners own the majority interest. However, the general partners retain the complete responsibility and control of managing the partnership business. Remember that a general partner also is exposed to unlimited liability for any partnership debts. Accordingly, it is prudent to avoid using an individual as a general partner, which would expose that individual to unlimited liability due to partnership activities. Normally, an entity that provides asset protection to the general partners will be used, such as an "S" corporation or limited liability company ("LLC").

Limited partners should have no control over the partnership and have no management rights in the partnership. The estate planning objective of the FLP is to "freeze" asset values and shift ownership of future asset growth from senior family members to junior family members. By virtue of creating a properly structured FLP, the senior family members have discounted the value of their interests in those assets used to fund the FLP, due to the valuation discounts referenced above, and have further created a platform for gift giving of limited partnership interest that will also be subject to valuation discounts for minority interests and lack-of-marketability. Thus, the FLP creates gift-giving leverage.

Do federal and state securities laws apply to FLPs?

Quite simply, a limited partnership interest is considered a "security" under the federal and Florida statutory definitions of "security". *Stowell v. Ted S. Finkle Investment Services, Inc., 489 F.Supp. 1290 (S.D. Fla. 1980); §4(2) of the Securities Act of 1933, 15 USC §§ 77(a) et seq.*

In order to avoid registration requirements, both Florida and federal law provide for a private placement exemption for the required registration of securities, including the sale or issuance of limited partnership interests. *Reg. D 17 CFR §§ 230.501 et seq; §517.061 (11)(a), Fla.Stat.* Even though a limited partnership interest may not be offered through a public offering, the anti-fraud and civil liability provisions of the *Securities Act of 1933 and Chapter 517, Fla.Stat.*, mandate full and fair disclosure of all material information regarding the investment in the FLP do apply.

When the FLP is created, each partner should execute an "investment letter" and a subscription agreement that represents: (a) that the investor is an accredited investor or has such knowledge and experience in financial and business matters that he or she is capable of evaluating the risk and merits of the investments; (b) that the partner understands that an investment involves a high degree of risk and that there is a potential to lose the entire investment; (c) that the investor was given the opportunity to ask questions and receive information from the general partner; (d) that the investor understands that the limited partnership interest have not been registered under the *Securities Act of 1933* ; and (e) that there will be restrictions on transferability of the interest for an indefinite period of time and that the investor is acquiring the interest for his or her own account and not for the account of others and for investment purposes only and not with the present intention to re-sell.

Under *Fla.Adm.Code §3E-500.005*, there are two options for full and fair disclosure necessary for the private placement exemption that apply under Florida law. One option is that the investors are provided reasonable access to and have been furnished with all material, books and records of the issuer, all material contracts and documents relating to the proposed transaction and an opportunity to question the appropriate executive officers or partners of the entity. The second option is to provide an offering circular prior to sale to the prospective investor that provides information as to a specific listing of twenty-eight items referenced therein and required by *§517.06 (11)(a)(3), Fla.Stat.*

What are the required formalities to form a limited partnership in Florida?

Even though a limited partnership may be in writing or created by oral agreement pursuant to *§620.102(9), Fla.Stat.*, prudence dictates that the limited partnership agreement be in writing since this agreement will govern the conduct and operation of the partnership business.

A certificate of limited partnership must be executed by all general partners to form a limited partnership pursuant to *§620.108* and *620.114, Fla.Stat.*

An affidavit indicating the amount of capital contributed by each partner must accompany the filing of the certificate of limited partnership pursuant to *§620.108(1), Fla.Stat.*

In order to give legal life to the limited partnership, one signed copy of the certificate of limited partnership must be filed with the Florida Department of State. The limited partnership is considered formed at the time the certificate of limited partnership is filed unless a later date is specified in the certificate. There is a filing fee to be paid along with the filing of the certificate of limited partnership that is calculated currently as $7.00 per $1,000 of the anticipated amount of the limited partners' capital contributions. The minimum filing fee for an FLP is $52.50 and the maximum filing fee is $1,750.00. Please be aware that these fees, as well as all governmental fees, are subject to change.

The certificate of limited partnership is required to be amended within 30 days after any new general partner is admitted to the partnership, any general partner withdraws from the partnership, the partnership continues business after the withdrawal of a general partner or the partnership changes its name. *§620.109(2)(a), Fla.Stat.*

If a FLP is dissolved, a certificate of cancellation must be filed with the Department of State. *§620.113, Fla.Stat.*

All domestic limited partnerships authorized to transact business in Florida must file an annual report to renew their certificate of authority on forms provided by the Department of State on or before December 31st of each year.

What are the common elements of a limited partnership agreement?

The name of a limited partnership must contain the word "Limited" or its abbreviation "Ltd." *§620.13(1), Fla.Stat.* The name of a limited partnership may not contain the name of a limited partner unless that limited partner is also a general partner or the business of the limited partnership was carried on under that name before the admission of the limited partner. *§620.103(2), Fla.Stat.*

The FLP agreement normally contains a purpose clause. If it is desirable to limit the scope of authority of the general partners of the FLP, a more specific purpose should be inserted in the agreement.

The term of the FLP is not limited by statue. However, the term must be definite according to *§620.108, Fla.Stat.*

Capital contributions of a limited partner or a general partner may be in the form of cash property, services, promissory note, or other contractual obligation to contribute cash, property or to perform services in the future. *§620.135, Fla.Stat.*

The FLP agreement can provide for the general partners' ability to call all limited partners to make additional capital contributions to the FLP. *§620.136(1), Fla.Stat.* Failure of a partner to make a required capital contribution can result in forfeiture of that partner's partnership interest.

The FLP agreement typically addresses the allocation of profits and losses of the partnership and distribution of cash or other assets to the partners. In the absence of such an allocation agreement, profits, losses and distributions to partners will be allocated on the basis of the value of their capital contributions to the partnership. *§620.137-620.138, Fla.Stat.* The FLP agreement can provide for a preferred pay-out of cash flow to the limited partners. However, any preferential pay-out of cash flow or other assets must pass the test of *IRC §704* and the accompanying regulations. If preferential allocations of profits and losses do not have "substantial economic effect", tax problems will result.

The FLP agreement should identify the fiscal year used and the method of accounting used by the partnership. A limited partnership must maintain a registered office where certain partnership records are kept. *§620.106(1), Fla.Stat.* Every domestic limited partnership that owns real property in Florida must maintain a registered office and a registered agent in Florida. *§620.192, Fla.Stat.*

To what extent is a FLP an effective asset protection planning strategy?

FLPs have a limited value as an asset protection strategy. First of all, a general partner is exposed to unlimited liability emanating from the operation of the partnership business. Secondly, personal creditors of a general partner may seize the general partner's interest or share of partnership income. Typically, the general partner seeks to insulate himself or herself from personal liability by transferring his or her general partnership interest to a subchapter "S" corporation or other entity with limited liability features.

A limited partner has liability to partnership creditors only to the extent of his or her interest in the partnership as far as his or her capital contribution is concerned. Personal creditors of a limited partner may obtain a charging order against a limited partner's income or foreclose on a limited partner's interest.

However, a Court does have the power to set aside any partnership interest that was created by virtue of a fraudulent conveyance according to state law.

If real estate is transferred to a FLP, is that transfer subject to the Florida documentary stamp tax?

Unfortunately, it is true that *§201.02, Fla.Stat.* and *Fla.Adm.Code §12B-4.013(10)* imposes a documentary stamp tax on the fair market value of real estate transferred to an FLP.

When will the tax status of an FLP be considered abusive by the Internal Revenue Service?

In January of 1995, the Internal Revenue Service (IRS) adopted the so-called "Anti-Abuse Rules" for partnerships that were published as proposed *Reg. §1.701-2,* as published on May 17, 1994, by the U.S. Treasury. Under this regulation, the IRS can disregard the partnership if the partnership was formed primarily to reduce the aggregate partnership liability in a manner inconsistent with the underlying economic arrangements.

Quite simply, if the only reason for the partnership is to reduce taxes, the arrangement will be considered abusive. For the FLP to avoid being classified as "abusive", it is necessary that the partnership have a substantial business purpose. In addition, the substance of each partnership transaction must be respected under the substance over form principal and the partnership transactions must accurately reflect the partners' economic agreement and properly reflect partner incomes.

The regulation lists seven factors which may indicate that the partnership abuses the partnership tax rules:

1. The aggregate tax liability is less than if the partners personally owned the assets.

2. The aggregate tax liability is less than if the purportedly separate transactions are integrated and treated as steps in a single transaction.

3. One or more partners needed to achieve the claimed tax results have only a nominal interest in the partnership.

4. Substantially all partners are related to one another.

5. Partnership items are allocated in compliance with the literal language but results are inconsistent with the intent of the regulations.

6. The partners contributing property to the partnership substantially retain its benefits and burdens.

7. The benefits and burdens of partnership property are substantially shifted to the distributee partner before or after the property is actually distributed to the distributee or a related party.

Is an interest in a limited partnership which is not publicly traded subject to the state intangible tax?

No. *§199.185(1)(c), Fla.Stat.*

Under what conditions can a gift of a limited partnership interest fail to qualify for the annual gift tax exclusion provide for in Code §2503(b)?

In *TAM 9751003*, the IRS ruled that gifts of limited partnership interest made by the donor failed to confer upon the donee the substantial present economic enjoyment requirement under *Code §2503(b)* for a present interest and as a result these gifts did not qualify for the gift tax annual exclusion provided for in that code section.

In the facts of this case, the IRS took position that the partnership agreement gave the general partner complete discretion over distribution of income and authorized the general partner to retain funds for any reason whatsoever.

Accordingly, the IRS held that such a provision negates any fiduciary duty ordinarily imposed upon a general partner and as a consequence the income component of the limited partnership interest failed to require, at the time of the gifts, that there be a steady and ascertainable flow of income to the donee/limited partner. The income component, therefore was not a present interest within the meaning of *Code §2503(b).* In order to avoid this result, the partnership agreement should provide that the general partner's discretion regarding distribution of income is subject to a fiduciary duty to the limited partners.

In *TAM 975 1003*, the IRS further determined that the capital component was not a present interest due to the existence of restrictions in the limited partnership agreement that prohibited limited partners from assigning their interest, withdrawing from the partnership or receiving a return of capital contributions until the partnership is terminated.

Is the distributive share of any item of income from an FLP to a limited partner subject to self-employment tax?

Under *IRC §1402(a)(13)*, the distributive share of income for an FLP to a limited partner is not considered within the definition of net earnings from self-employment income and therefore not subject to self-employment tax, except for guaranteed payments under *IRC §707(c).*

Can an FLP act as an alternate entity to own life insurance?

Interestingly enough, an FLP can serve as an alternative planning strategy to an irrevocable life insurance trust (ILIT). An FLP can provide some advantages not available in an ILIT. FLP's can provide the insured greater control over the policy, are not subject to the Crummey withdrawal power requirements and may provide flexibility not possible in an ILIT. If the insured is a general partner, only the discounted value of his or her interest in the partnership will be included in his or her estate. *Rev. Rul. 83-147; IRC §2033, Reg. Sec. 20.2031-3.* An FLP that owns only life insurance is considered a valid partnership under *IRC §7701. Pvt.Ltr.Rul. 9309021.*

How has the Strangi line of cases affected FLP planning?

The *Strangi* cases, supra, have radically altered FLP planning and have given everyone who has created or intends to create a FLP to pause and give some serious thought as to the viability of the FLP concept in light of the *Strangi* cases.

In *Strangi III,* the U.S. Tax Court held that the full fair market value of assets owned by a FLP were includable in the decedent's taxable estate, as of the date of death, thus totally ignoring the FLP entity valuation discounts, due to the decedent's retained interests as to FLP distrubutions of FLP income (or other FLP assets) and as a result of the decedent's control over transferred FLP assets. This holding was based upon the application of *IRC Sections 2036 (a)(1) and (a)(2),* which has been the latest and most successful avenue of legal attack of FLPs by the IRS.

This ruling has sent shock waves through the FLP planning world and shivers through attorneys, CPAs and clients alike who have, or intend to create, FLPs. The *Strangi III* case compels the review of existing FLPs in light of the *IRC § 2036* theory of IRS attack against FLPs and has consequently imposed a new prism of required analysis for prospective FLPs considering the application of the *Strangi III* rationale.

First, we shall review the *Strangi III* case reasoning in this article and then we will consider what remedial or alternate planning options may exist to address the FLP planning implications of *Strangi III.*

IRC § 2036(a)(1) provides that a decedent's estate is to include the full fair market value of all property transferred by a decedent during his or her lifetime to a trust *or otherwise* wherein the said transferor decedent has retained "the possession or enjoyment of, or the right to income from" from such transferred property for his or her life. The statutory term "enjoyment" essentially means the retention by the decedent of a substantial present economic benefit, such as the ability of the transferor to retain control of entity income either formally or through implied agreement for his or her benefit. cf. *Estate of McNichol v. Commissioner, 265 F. 2d 667 (3d Cir. 1959)*; Estate of Reichardt v. Commissioner, supra; Estate of Thompson v. Commissioner, supra.

IRC § 2036(a)(2) provides that the full fair market value of property transferred by a decedent during the decedent's lifetime to a trust *or otherwise* is included in the decedent transferor's estate if the decedent transferor retained "the right, either alone or in conjunction with others, to designate the persons" who will have beneficial enjoyment of the transferred property. The statutory term "right" has been defined to mean "an ascertainable or legally enforceable power" in the *Strangi III* case. cf. U.S. v. Byrum, *408 U.S. 125 (1972)*.

The facts involved in the *Strangi III* case are as follows:

Albert Strangi (referred to as "Strangi" or the "decedent") was a wealthy businessman who had four children from a first marriage and two stepchildren from a second marriage. Strangi developed a serious brain disorder in 1993. Previously, in 1988, Strangi had given his son-in-law, Michael J. Gullig, a power of attorney to act on his behalf. Mr. Gullig was an attorney. In July of 1990, Strangi executed a Will that devised the residue of his estate to his four children if his wife predeceased him. Mrs. Strangi died five months later.

As Strangi's health declined, Mr. Gullig became closer to him and Mr. Gullig assumed a position of Strangi's closest advisor and confidant.

In August of 1994, Mr. Gullig attended a Fortress Financial Group ("Fortress") seminar on FLPs. Mr. Gullig then formed a Texas FLP named the Strangi Family Limited Partnership ("SFLP") with a corporate general partner ("STRANCO") utilizing Fortress forms. Mr. Gullig then capitalized SFLP with 98% of Strangi's assets valued at $9,876,929 in exchange for a 99% limited partnership interest for Strangi. The assets transferred consisted of mostly cash and securities, but also included real estate, Strangi's residence, life insurance, an annuity, receivables and other business interests in partnerships. Mr. Gullig bought a 47% interest in STRANCO for Strangi with the balance of STRANCO being purchased by Mrs. Gullig and her three siblings. STRANCO contributed $100,333 to SFLP in exchange for a 1% general partner's interest in SFLP. Later, on August 18, 1994, the Strangi children transferred a 1% interest in STRANCO to the McLennan Community College Foundation ("MCCF"). On October 14, 1994, Strangi died. Since September of 1993, Strangi had required 24/7 home health care by nursing services and he needed a housekeeper since he could not care for himself. SFLP funds were used to pay for personal living expenses of the decedent and after Strangi's death, SFLP funds were used to pay for the decedent's debts, funeral expenses, probate administrative expenses, fund a specific devise to the decedent's sister and to pay for estate taxes of $3,187,800.

Strangi's estate tax return represented the following:

1. Gross estate value was $6,823,582.

2. A 33% discount was taken for lack of marketability and lack of control of SFLP.

3. Decedent's SFLP interest was valued at $6,560,730 and his interest in STRANCO was valued at $24,551.

4. The fair market value of the SFLP assets were $11,100,922 at the time of death.

After audit, the IRS contended that Strangi's SFLP intetest should have been valued at $10,947,343 and his STRANCO interest should have been valued at $53,560.

In the *Strangi I* case, the Tax Court ruled against the IRS position that was based upon the contentions that SFLP was not a valid FLP under state law and that *IRC § 2703* applied. The IRS sought leave to amend its answer to include a *IRC § 2036* argument and the Tax Court denied the request as untimely. The IRS appealed to the Fifth Circuit and the Court remanded the case to the Tax Court with instructions to consider whether *IRC § 2036* applies and to explain why the IRS motion to amend was denied in more detail. This decision is referred to as the *Strangi II* case. Upon remand, the Tax Court rendered the *Strangi III* decision.

In *Strangi III*, the Tax Court found that Mr. Gullig acted on behalf of Strangi with his full authority and thus Strangi maintained sole discretion over the FLP assets. The Tax Court found that Strangi maintained (through an implied agreement with Mr. Gulig) control over distribution of FLP income and assets while retaining possession and enjoyment of the assts he transferred to fund SFLP. This triggered the application of *IRC § 2036(a)(1)*. In such finding, the Tax Court listed the following facts: (a) Strangi transferred most of his assets (98%) to SFLP; (b) Strangi continued to live in his residence that was transferred to SFLP; (c) Rent was accrued but not collected for use of the residence; (d) SFLP assets were used to pay for Strangi's personal expenses; (e) the entire plan was testamentary in nature.

The Tax Court also held that *IRC § 2036(a)(2)* applied to the facts of the case since Strangi retained the right to designate who shall possess or enjoy the property transferred by Strangi to fund SFLP. The Tax Court found that Strangi retained the authority, either alone or through his attorney, to control SFLP distributions and to terminate the FLP and, accordingly, the decedent could control the enjoyment of the assets transferred to SFLP.

As a side issue, the Tax Court held that the transfers by the decedent to SFLP were not to be considered a bona fide sale thus not subject to the exception provided for in *IRC Section 2036(a)(2)* that states that said Code Section does not apply in the case of a bona fide sale for adequate consideration in money or money's worth. cf. <u>Estate of Jones v. Commissioner</u>, *121 T.C. 116 (2001)*; <u>Estate of Church v. United States</u>, *268 F. 3d 1063 (2001).*

The Tax Court said that IRC *§* 2036(a)(2) is applicable in the *Strangi* case due to the fact that Strangi had the legally enforceable right, directly or indirectly, to control SFLP distributions and Strangi, as the sole limited partner, had the legally enforceable right to join with the general partner of SFLP to cause a termination and liquidation of the partnership. The Tax Court held that the case of <u>U.S. v. Byrum, 408 U.S. 125</u> *(1972)* did not apply to prevent inclusion.

It is fair to say that due to the application of the *Strangi III* case rationale, other entities such as corporations and LLCs would be subject to the same *Strangi* case reasoning. From an entity planning perspective, it can be speculated that if a client forms a FLP (or other entity) and that client retains control over distribution of entity assets or can control, directly or indirectly, the power to liquidate the entity, then you can expect the IRS position to be that any assets transferred to capitalize said entity by the client will be sought to be included back into the client's estate upon death pursuant to the *IRC § 2036 (a)* position successfully argued in the *Strangi III* case. The *Strangi III* case can be interpreted to also mean that FLP units previously gifted away will *de facto* be included in the decedent's estate since the underlying FLP asset values will be included in the transferor's estate. The bottom line lesson of *Strangi III* may well be that if the transferor decedent holds the authority or power, either alone or with another, to control or participate in FLP asset distribution or liquidation decisions, expressly or impliedly, then *IRC § 2036 (a)* shall operate to cause inclusion of all underlying FLP assets that were transferred to the FLP as valued as of the date of the transferor's death. Ouch indeed! See discussion in article, *Strangi: A Critical Analysis and Planning Suggestions* by Mitchell M. Gans and Jonathan G. Blattmachr, *Tax Analysis Special Report, Tax Notes* © September 1, 2003.

There are four other recent Tax Court cases (*Estate of Schauerhamer v. Commissioner; Estate of Reichardt v. Commissioner; Estate of Harper v. Commissioner; Estate of Thompson v. Commissioner, supra*) and one U.S. District Court case (*Kimbell v. United States, supra*) that dealt with *IRC § 2036* inclusion issues and involved findings of express or implied agreements or understandings between decedent transferors to FLPs and other partners wherein the decedent transferor retained "enjoyment" or "economic benefit" from assets transferred to the FLP.

In the *Schauerhamer, Reichardt, Harper* and *Thompson* decisions, the Tax Court found that an implied agreement or understanding existed between the decedent transferor and the other FLP partners that resulted in the decedent transferor retaining lifetime control of FLP assets that was prohibited by *IRC § 2036 (a)(1)*.

In *Kimbell,* the trial court found that the actual partnership agreement at issue provided: (a) limitless discretionary power for the decedent transferor to determine FLP distributions of FLP assets; (b) authority to remove the general partner at the decedent's whim; (c) that the general partner of the FLP had no fiduciary duties to the other partners; and (d) that the decedent transferor dictated possession and enjoyment of FLP assets. Such agreement terms triggered the application of *IRC § 2036(a)* to cause inclusion of FLP assets. However, the Fifth Circuit Court of Appeals recently vacated the trial court's decision that rejected the IRS attack in this case based upon the above Code section and remanded the case back to the trial court.

Another point raised by the above cases involves the application of the holding of the case, *United States v. Grace, 395 U.S. 316(1969)*, that stands for the proposition that *IRC § 2036 (a)* applies to transfers that are "testamentary in nature". cf. Ray v. United States, 762 U.S. 1361, 1362 (9th Cir. 1985); Guynn v. United States, 437 F. 2d 1148, 1150 (4th Cir. 1971).

The estate planning implications of the *Strangi III, Kimbell* and other "2036" cases referenced above seem to indicate that where a transferor senior family member creates a FLP and retains any express or implied authority or powers that result in transferor control over FLP income or assets, then inclusion of the FLP assets will occur in the transferor's estate at his or her death.

However, this is not to say that there are no positive FLP cases that have been recently decided. cf. *Estate of Stone v Commissioner, T.C. Memo 2003-309; Wheeler v. Commissioner, 116 F. 3d 749 (5th Cir. 1997)*. In *Stone*, the Tax Court agreed with the taxpayer position that relied upon the "bona fide sale and adequate exception" contained in *IRC § 2036(a)* in a FLP scenario.

What about the Kimbell case and its application to FLP planning?

As indicated above, the Fifth Circuit Court of Appeals on May 20, 2004, vacated and remanded the *Kimbell* case, supra, to the trial court to determine values of certain assets and proceedings consistent with the Fifth Circuit's ruling that *IRC § 2036(a)* did not apply in the case. Let's review this decision since it was a big IRS defeat on the FLP inclusion issue.

First, let's look briefly at the facts of the *Kimbell* case. At first blush, the facts did not look good for the taxpayer since the factual scenario involved a "deathbed" FLP. Mrs. Kimbell formed a Texas FLP at the age of 96 just two months prior to her death. The FLP was owned as follows. The 1% FLP general partner was a LLC that was 50% owned by Mrs. Kimbell's revocable trust and 50% owned by the decedent's son and daughter-in-law. The 99% limited partner's interest was owned 100% by Mrs. Kimbell's revocable trust. The decedent's revocable trust contributed \$2,534,225.80 for a 99% limited partner's interest and the LLC contributed \$25,342.26 in cash for a 1% general partner's interest in the FLP. The assets contributed by the decedent's revocable trust consisted of over 80% of liquid assets, i.e. cash, marketable securities, and family note receivables.

The federal district court held that all FLP assets were includable in the decedent's estate pursuant to *IRC § 2036(a)(1) and (2)*, as contended by the IRS.

The Fifth Circuit disagreed with the trial court and reversed holding that Mrs. Kimbell's transfers of assets to the FLP constituted "bona fide sales for full and adequate consideration", thus fell within the bona fide sale exception under *IRC §*

2036. In essence, the court said that Mrs. Kimbell exchanged her assets for partnership interests of roughly equivalent value and that the objective facts of the case indicated that the transaction was "bona fide" or genuine. The court said that the test for adequate and full consideration as set forth in the *Estate of Stone* case, supra, was satisfied by the taxpayer in *Kimbell*, to-wit: (1) whether the interests credited to each of the partners was proportionate to the fair market value of the assets each partner contributed to the partnership; (2) whether the assets contributed by each partner to the partnership were properly credited to the respective capital accounts of the partners, and; (3) whether on termination or dissolution of the partnership the partners were entitled to distributions from the partnership in amounts equal to their respective capital accounts.

The Fifth Circuit found that there were five important facts that supported the holding that the transfer of assets to the FLP by *Kimbell* constituted a "bona fide sale", to-wit:

1. Sufficient assets outside the FLP were retained by Mrs. Kimbell for her support.

2. There was no commingling of Mrs. Kimbell's personal and FLP assets.

3. Partnership assets were transferred to the FLP and the FLP maintained requisite statutory formalities.

4. FLP assets required active management (13% of assets transferred to FLP were oil and gas working interests).

5. There were non-tax reasons for transfer.

The court further indicated that Mrs. Kimbell did not retain sufficient control over the FLP assets via the general partner LLC due to her having only a 50% interest in the LLC and her son had sole managerial control over the LLC.

The *Strangi II* case is pending before the Fifth Circuit with briefs to be filed soon. The saga continues.

What are some problems to be alert to when creating or operating FLPs in light of recent case law ?

There are a variety of problematic FLP factual scenarios that are critical to identify and address when creating or operating an existing FLP such as:

The FLP agreement and related documents should be drafted (and filed if required) in accordance with controlling state law.

Avoid transferring the majority of transferor's assets to the FLP and avoid transferring personal assets, i.e. residence, personal auto, etc., to the FLP.

Avoid pre-packaged form FLP agreements, ex. The Fortress Financial Group forms as used in *Strangi* case. Utilize competent legal counsel to plan and draft FLP documents.

Avoid giving controlling FLP powers over income and FLP assets to transferor senior family members that are violative of *IRC § 2036* that cause inclusion of FLP assets in transferor's estate as per *Strangi III* case rationale.

Avoid giving transferor senior family members sole discretion to control, remove and replace the FLP general partner.

Avoid FLP creation where transferor is in poor health, very elderly or terminally ill.

Avoid nullification of general partner's fiduciary duties to limited partners in the FLP agreement.

Use "IRS defendable" business valuation of FLP interests gifted away.

Avoid the transferor's personal use of FLP assets that disregard the legal integrity of the FLP. Clearly separate management of FLP assets from personal assets.

Have a true business purpose for the FLP.

The FLP should achieve planning objectives other than transfer tax reduction and accomplishing testamentary transfers to junior family members.

Avoid implied control agreements where transferor retains power to directly or indirectly control FLP income distributions or enjoyment of FLP assets.

Avoid giving transferor first option to receive FLP income or asset distributions.

Comply with annual state law filing requirements for the FLP and adhere to keeping required FLP books and records. Keep separate FLP bank accounts and avoid commingling of funds.

Avoid disproportionate FLP distributions to senior family members for personal living expenses, medical expenses, personal family gifts, loans to junior family members and providing free use of FLP assets to senior family members.

FLP assets should always be titled in FLP name.

Beware of senior family member control of FLP assets via indirect means or through implied agreements wit junior family members.

Senior family member majority ownership of FLP continues with few or no transfers of FLP interests until death.

FLP is administered more like trust than business entity.

FLP formalities are disregarded. FLP partners not compensated for services rendered to FLP nor is adequate return on FLP investment occurring. Avoid disproportionate partner distributions that do not correlate with economic realities.

Avoid "off the shelf" boilerplate FLP documents sold by FLP promoters.

Avoid creating FLP for very sick, mentally incompetent or very elderly senior family member; especially "deathbed" FLPs.

Tax avoidance should not be the sole reason for the FLP. There must be legitimate non-tax, business reasons for forming the FLP. Do not transfer most of senior family member's assets into the FLP. Do not capitalize FLP with only cash and securities.

Have all partners represented by competent legal counsel and CPAs so that all legal and tax ramifications of the FLP can be discussed by the partners prior to setting up the FLP.

What FLP planning strategies can be employed to avoid the effect of the Strangi III case?

The *Strangi III* case discussed above rests upon the applicability of *IRC §'s 2036(a)(1) and (2)*. Therefore, pursuant to the effect of said statutes, the FLP structure must not create a right on the part of the senior family member transferor to: (a) retain the right to income, possession or enjoyment of the FLP assets; or, (b) retain the right to designate possession or enjoyment of FLP assets. Set forth below are suggested strategies that may be used to avoid *Strangi III* inclusion issues. CAVEAT: Do not view these suggested tactics as Gospel; get your own independent legal and tax advice that fits your case.

In order to avoid the *IRC § 2036(a)(1)* inclusion problem: (1) Significant personal assets should be maintained outside the FLP for the benefit of the transferor; (2) Personal assets should not be transferred to the FLP; (3) Other FLP partners, i.e. junior family members, should contribute capital to the FLP; (4) The general partner should not be (nor directly or indirectly controlled by an entity or implied agreement with the transferor) the transferor senior family member; (5) Gifts of FLP interests by transferor senior family members to junior family members should regularly occur to avoid testamentary characterization by IRS; (6) The FLP should be operated as a real business with the intent to earn a profit.

In order to avoid *IRC § 2036(a)(2)* inclusion problem: (1) Do not make the primary transferor senior family member the general partner (or have him or her control the general partner); (2) Avoid implicit or implied agreements that cause the primary transferor to retain control of FLP assets, either directly or indirectly; (3) Transfer FLP units to trust that has independent trustee; (4) As a remedial tactic, have the primary transferor make gifts (or sell) of FLP units to relinquish control; (5) Reorganize the FLP into two or more FLPs in order to divide assets between the partners and therefore address control issues; (6) Amend the FLP agreement to avoid problematic terms that cause inclusion; (7) Sell or gift FLP units to eliminate control problem.

Chapter III
LLCs as a Planning Tool

What is a limited liability company?

When considering the selection of a private business entity ownership structure for a business in Florida, there are a variety of potential choices under Florida law, to-wit: corporations (either "S" or "C" tax status), limited partnerships ("LPs"), limited liability partnerships ("LLPs"), limited liability limited partnerships ("LLLPs"), business trusts (also known as common-law declarations of trust under *Chapter 609, Florida Statutes*), general partnerships or limited liability companies ("LLCs").

A LLC is a hybrid business entity in that it has the limited liability protection for its owners (that are identified as "members" in a LLC) analogous to shareholders/owners of corporations while otherwise being treated as a partnership for income tax purposes.

The LLC entity-style concept has been around for some time. Many countries around the world have long-standing LLC-type statutes and every state in the U.S. has adopted a form of LLC statutes. Wyoming was the first state to adopt a LLC act in the U.S. that was modeled after the German GmBH statute. In 1982, Florida followed by adopting its LLC statutes. However, LLCs were not widely used in Florida until the IRS enacted the "Check-the-Box" Treasury Regulations in 1997 that allowed automatic treatment of LLCs as a partnership for income tax purposes (and which repealed the "Kintner" regulations for business entity tax classification purposes) and the state of Florida repealed the application of Florida's 5.5% corporate income tax to LLCs after July 1, 1998. cf. *§§608.471, 220.11 and 220.13(2)(j), Florida Statutes.*

In 1993, the Florida LLC statutes were amended to permit professional LLCs and allow corporate characteristics for LLCs. Other changes have occurred with respect to the Florida LLC law that have made Florida LLCs more attractive as an entity of choice, for example:

1. A LLC can have one or more members. *§608.405, Florida Statutes.*

2. A LLC member can be any person or entity, foreign or domestic. *§§608.402(21) Florida Statutes.*

3. A LLC can be formed by filing articles of organization filed by one member or an authorized representative. *§608.407(3), Florida Statutes.*

4. Capital contributions of a member can consist of cash, property, services rendered or to be rendered, a promissory note or other obligation to contribute cash or property. *§608.4211(1), Florida Statutes.*

5. A LLC can be a member-managed LLC or a manager-managed LLC. *§608.422, Florida Statutes.*

6. A member's LLC interest is subject to a charging order obtained against the member/judgment debtor by a judgment creditor which limits the judgment creditor to being an assignee of the member's LLC profit distributions, if any. *§608.433(4), Florida Statutes.*

7. There can be different classes of members with or without various rights as a LLC member, including voting rights. *§608.4231, Florida Statutes.*

As a consequence of the above-noted federal tax law and Florida law changes affecting LLCs, now LLCs have become a prominent business entity choice.

How may a LLC be taxed?

It is typical that LLC members wish to be taxed as a partnership for federal income tax and Florida corporate income tax purposes if such members wish for the LLC to be a "pass-through" entity and be subject to partnership tax rules. Pursuant to the "Check-the-Box" Treasury Regulations that became effective as of January 1, 1997, the default tax classification of a LLC is that a LLC is considered a partnership for income tax treatment purposes. *Reg. 301.7701-1, et. seq.; Rev. Proc. 95-10.* However, if the entity is a single-member LLC, then the LLC shall be automatically defaulted to having a "sole proprietorship" tax status, i.e. the member reports LLC activities on his or her Schedule C in their respective Form 1040. *Reg. 301.7701-2(c)(1).* Therefore, it is important to distinguish multiple-member LLCs from single-member LLCs for tax classification reasons.

Moreover, LLC members can elect out of the "Check-the-Box" regulations tax default classification. In a multiple-member LLC, i.e. a LLC with two or more members, the members can elect "C" corporation or "S" corporation tax status by filing Form 8832 and Form 2553 (if "S" corporation status is elected). In a single-member LLC, the member may similarly elect "C" corporation or "S" corporation status.

Thus, in light of the available tax elections possible, a LLC can be an extremely flexible tax planning entity choice. However, remember that the LLC operating agreement should conform with the tax status chosen in order to avoid possibly unintended negative tax consequences.

The new "Check-the-Box Regulations" make it easy to now classify a LLC for federal tax purposes. Beware that a single member LLC cannot be classified a "partnership" for federal income tax purposes. *Reg.Sec.301.7701-2(c)(1).*

Regardless of the number of "corporate characteristics" a LLC may have, ex. perpetual life, centralized management, limited liability for owners or free transferability of interests, the LLC may elect to be taxed as a partnership. These new regulations create certainty in the federal income tax treatment of LLCs and make compliance easier.

Due to the applicable "Check-the-Box" regulations, all uncertainty has been removed with respect to how LLCs are to be taxed.

How is a LLC formed and operated?

In order to form a LLC, one must file articles of organization with the Florida Department of State office along with the requisite filing fees (currently $125.00, including registered agent's fee). There is a required annual report filing for Florida LLCs (currently a $50.00 fee). Pursuant to *§608.407, Florida Statutes*, LLC articles of organization must include:

1. The LLC name that shall be identified as "limited liability company", "limited company', "L.L.C.", "LLC", "L.C." or "LC".

2. The mailing address and street address of the LLC.

3. The name and Florida address of the registered agent of the LLC along with his or her signature of acceptance.

4. A description of LLC as a member-managed company, if that is the case.

5. Articles must be signed by at least one member or authorized representative.

6. If an effective date is listed, the date must be specific and cannot be more than five business days prior to or ninety days after the date of filing.

LLC owners are called "members". Unless otherwise stated in articles or operating agreement, LLC s are deemed to be member-managed. *§608.422(1), Florida Statutes*. A LLC can be manager-managed. *§608.422(3), Florida Statutes*. Different classes of members can be created in a LLC, e.g. voting and non-voting classes of members. *§608.4231, Florida Statutes*. Thus, a LLC could be set up analogous to a limited partnership in that the LLC could be managed by one or more managing members (or non-member manager) that would be the equivalent of a general partner in a limited partnership while other members could be passive, non-voting members who would be the equivalent of limited partners.

A member's ownership interest in a LLC can be physically represented by a LLC certificate that is analogous to stock certificates in a corporation. These certificates can express ownership as number of units or as percentage of ownership in the LLC.

The operating agreement of a LLC that is signed by all members is the internal governing document of the LLC. The operating agreement includes rules and regulations pertaining to scheduling of meetings of members, voting rights of members, fiscal matters, management authority, distribution of profits of losses, maintenance of books and records of LLC, appointment of operating manager or other officers, restriction on sale or transfer of member interests and other operational issues.

A member-managed LLC is managed by vote of its members like a general partnership. A manager-managed LLC is managed by its manager(s) like a limited partnership. Each manager or managing member owes a duty of loyalty and a duty of care to both the LLC and its members. *§608.4225, Florida Statutes*.

What is the liability exposure of a LLC member?

Members of a LLC are not personally liable for debts, obligations, judgments or other non-personally guaranteed liabilities of the LLC. *§608.4227, Florida Statutes*. However, members are liable for return of improper distributions of LLC assets. *§608.426, Florida Statutes*. It is an open question whether "piercing the corporate veil" type of theories of liability will be successful against LLC members. Logically, such theories of liability would be applicable if: (a) the LLC incurred debt while insolvent; (b) the members did not adhere to statutory formalities for setting up or operating a LLC; (c) the legal form of the LLC was disregarded by members; (d) members commingled LLC assets; (e) the LLC was used to perpetrate a fraud; or (f) the LLC was used merely as an "alter-ego" of the members.

What is the exposure of a LLC member's interest to a third party creditor?

A LLC member's interest can be attacked by his or her judgment creditor only through the use of a "charging order". *§608.433(4), Florida Statutes*. A charging order is obtained by a judgment creditor of the LLC member upon application to a court of competent jurisdiction. The charging order requires the LLC to make LLC distributions due to the member to the judgment creditor instead until the judgment is satisfied. However, a charging order does not require the LLC to make any such distributions to the LLC member/judgment debtor and therein lies the rub for the judgment creditor. The judgment creditor has the rights of an assignee with respect to the LLC member's interest and, thus, if there are no LLC distributions, the creditor gets nothing. This legal reality would then supposedly motivate the settlement of the creditor's judgment.

There has been no case law in Florida adjudicating whether a charging order is the exclusive remedy of a judgment creditor against a LLC member/judgment debtor. However, both federal and state courts in Florida have held that a charging order is the exclusive remedy for a judgment creditor versus a limited partner/judgment debtor in a limited partnership, thus preventing the execution sale of limited partnership interests in order to satisfy a judgment obtained against the limited partner. *Matter of Dutch Inn of Orlando, Ltd., 2 B.R. 268 (Bankr. M.D. Fla. 1980); Pressner v. Pressner, 59 So.2d 379 (Fla. 2d DCA 1991); Givens v. National Loan Investors, L.P., 724 So.2d 610 (Fla. 5th DCA 1999*). The charging order remedy statute for limited partnerships is pretty much the same in terms of intent as the LLC statute. *§620.153, Florida Statutes*. From the current status of the law in Florida, we can presume that the charging order now appears to be the exclusive remedy for judgment creditors who seek collection of his or her judgment against a LLC member.

Can LLCs be used in professional practices?

Pursuant to *Chapter 621, Florida Statutes*, a professional such as an attorney, CPA, etc., and their respective professional service corporations or other entities, can organize a "professional limited liability company" in order to render professional services. *§621.03(3), Florida Statutes*. Non-licensed persons cannot utilize a professional LLC. *§621.06, Florida Statutes*. Professional liability, i.e. malpractice, accrues to the professional (or by the person under that person's supervision and control) committing the negligence while performing services on behalf of the LLC. The assets of the LLC are also subject to the claims of a malpractice plaintiff, regardless of who committed the malpractice. *§621.07, Florida Statutes*. Only professionals licensed in the same profession can form a professional LLC. The name of a professional LLC must contain suffix "Chartered" or "P.L.". *§621.12, Florida Statutes*.

Interestingly enough, a CPA can form a non-professional LLC to engage in the accounting practice if the LLC complies with *§473.309(3), Florida Statutes*.

Is the transfer of appreciated property to capitalize a LLC a taxable event?

Gain is not generally recognized when a LLC member transfers appreciated property in exchange for his or her LLC interest. *Internal Revenue Code ("Code") §721(a).* This non-recognition rule is subject to the "investment company" exception. *Code §721(b).* If a LLC member transfers appreciated property that results in "diversification" and, after the exchange, more than 80% of the LLC assets constitute "stock and securities", then the transfer creates a taxable event. *Reg. §1.351-1(c)(1).* "Stock and securities" are defined in *Code §351(e)(1)(B).* Closely held business securities fall within the above definition.

What is the meaning of the above? The investment company problem becomes an issue only when different family members contribute different securities to capitalize the LLC. For reference, review *S.Rep.No. 938, 94th Cong., 2nd Sess. pt. 2, at 43-44(1976).*

How are LLC interests valued for transfer tax purposes?

LLCs can be used as a planning platform in order to make gifts to junior family members. Gifting of LLC interests require valuation of those interests for IRS reporting purposes. It can be said that business valuation is not a science but an art. This is due to the fact that business valuation is an opinion of fair market value ("FMV") that is subject to various factors. For estate and gift tax valuation purposes, FMV is the price at which property would change hands between a willing buyer and a willing seller with neither being under any compulsion to buy or to sell and both having reasonable knowledge of all relevant facts. *Reg. §20.2031-1(b);Reg. §25.2512-1.*

When a LLC interest is gifted by a senior family member to a junior family member, the valuation of the gifted interest may be subject to three types of discounts:

1. <u>Lack of Marketability Discount</u>. This discount results from the LLC interest not having an established market for sale and purchase.

2. <u>Minority Discount</u>. This discount results from the LLC interest not having control of the LLC business.

3. <u>Fractional Discount</u>. This discount results from the inconvenience of shared ownership and management.

Beware that if the gift of the LLC interest is intended to qualify for the

$11,000.00 per donee annual exclusion as per *Code §2503(b)*, the LLC operating agreement should contain the equivalent of at least a sixty (60) day "Crummey Power" provision that provides the donee member a restricted right to obtain the gifted asset or sell the gifted interest for a limited time period. cf. *Hackl v. Commissioner, 118 T.C. No. 14 (March 27, 2002); TAM 9751003.*

How is a "S" corporation different than a LLC for tax and estate planning purposes?

An "S" corporation is subject to various legal restrictions in terms of use that are not applicable to a LLC, ex. all shareholders of "S" corporation must be either U.S. citizens or U.S. resident aliens (*Code §1361(b)*), shareholders are limited to seventy-five (75) in an "S" corporation (*Code §1361(b)(1)(A)*), "S" corporations cannot retain or acquire "S" status if business activity is prohibited, e.g. bank, insurance company, foreign corporation, etc. (*Code §1361(b)(2)*), an "S" corporation can only have one class of stock (*Code §1361(b)(1)*), "S" corporation distributions of appreciated property to shareholders trigger taxable gain to corporation (*Code §1368*), shareholder's stock basis in "S" not increased when corporate debt is assumed (*Code §1367*), "S" corporations cannot specially allocate gains or losses among shareholders (*Code §1366(a)*) and shareholders of "S" corporations have no charging order type of asset protection.

Can an existing entity be converted into a LLC?

In *§608.439, Florida Statutes*, general partnerships, limited partnerships, business trusts, foreign LLCs, common-law trusts, real estate investment trusts or other unincorporated businesses can convert into a Florida LLC. When conversion occurs, title to real property (as well as other personalty owned by the entity) transfers to the new LLC without the need for recording a deed or paying state documentary stamp taxes.

How about cross-entity mergers?

Cross-entity mergers are permitted in Florida by filing a Certificate of Merger with the State. *§§608.438 - 608.4383, Florida Statutes.*

However, beware of tax consequences of merger! Merger of a "C" or "S" corporation into a LLC constitutes a corporate liquidation that results in a taxable event. Conversion of a partnership into a LLC should not be a taxable event. *Code §708; Treas. Regs. §1.708-1cc); Rev. Rul. 84-52, 1984-1 C.B. 157.*

Is a transfer of real property to capitalize a LLC subject to state documentary stamp taxes?

The Department of Revenue of the State of Florida takes the position under *F.A.C. §12B-4.013(7)* and *§201.02, Florida Statutes*, that when you transfer real property to a LLC in exchange for a LLC member interest, that is a transfer that is subject to the state documentary stamp tax of $.70 per $100.00 of value transferred. A Florida state court held in the case captioned *Kuro v. Florida Dept. of Revenue, 713 So.2d 1021 (Fla. 2nd DCA 1998)* that there is an exception to the above position so dearly maintained by the Department of Revenue. In *Kuro*, the taxpayers equally owned real property that was transferred for liability protection reasons to a new corporation in exchange for equal shares in said corporation. The court held in the *Kuro* case that there was no taxable purchase of real estate because the transferors did not receive anything different in terms of ownership in exchange, thus no documentary stamp taxes were due.

The *Kuro* case holding incited the Department of Revenue to attack that precedent by contesting the assessment of state documentary stamp taxes on a capitalization of a limited partnership by a corporate partner and two individual partners. The corporate partner contributed realty for a 98% interest and the individual partners contributed other dissimilar assets for a 2% interest. This factual scenario was deemed to generate a taxable transfer of real estate, i.e. documentary stamp taxes, due to different partners contributing different assets. *Muben-Lamar, L.P. v. Department of Revenue, 763 So. 2d 1209 (Fla. 1st DCA 2000)*. The Florida Supreme Court, in June 2001, decided that there was no conflict between *Kuro* and *Muben-Lamar* and thus declined to hear the appellate case.

It appears that for a transfer of real estate to fall within the *Kuro* case rationale, factually, the LLC must have pre-existed the transfer of realty and the ownership of the realty must have been the same as the ownership of the new LLC entity. LLC certificates should be issued prior to the transfer. The realty should not be mortgaged. The transfer of mortgaged realty to a LLC will result in document stamp tax liability to the extent of the unpaid mortgage encumbering the realty transferred. *Department of Revenue v. Race, 743 So.2d 169 (Fla. 5th DCA 1999).*

What are the general advantages of using a limited liability company business entity?

Creditor protection can be generated by using the LLC. LLC members have limited liability to the extent of capital contributed. LLC member interests can only be attacked by individual creditors to the extent of the "charging order". LLC members can manage business without personal liability.

Avoidance of double income tax at the state and federal level. LLC is taxed as partnership, if properly constructed, and therefore acts as “pass through” tax entity.

Family LLCs (“FLLCs”) offers flexible planning options. FLLCs can be used to accomplish “estate freezing” of values by creating multiple classes of voting and non-voting stock. FLLC interests can be transferred between family members in order to shift income and wealth.

Management of LLC can be centralized. Members of non-members can be used to fill management roles.

LLC can be used to consolidate wealth in one entity to provide economies of scale and centralized control of assets within the LLC.

LLC can be used to avoid ancillary probate.

LLC has all advantages of “flow through” or “pass through” tax entity, however, beware of loss deduction limitations imposed by *Code Sec. 469* and basis limitation rules.

LLC members can specially allocate income, gains, losses, credits and deductions to accomplish income shifting so long as allocations have substantial economic effect as per *Code Sec. 704.*

LLC members can convert passive losses into active losses or vice versa due to characterization of member.

LLC can generate multiple valuation discounts, i.e., lack of marketability and minority discounts, for estate tax planning purposes.

LLC can have individuals or any other legal entities as members. This facilitates financing businesses. Ideal for joint ventures. Ideal for holding or developing real property.

LLC members tax basis is increased by member’s proportionate share of recourse or non-recourse liabilities for entity.

LLC members can receive distributions of appreciated property from LLC without taxable gain at entity level or at member level if member has enough basis to absorb value of distribution.

LLCs can elect “S” or “C” corporation tax treatment and single-member LLCs can do likewise.

What are the relative disadvantages of a limited liability company?

LLCs lack extensive litigation history across the country.

Transfer of LLC interest subject to consent of other members.

LLC must have a substantial business or investment purpose in order to obtain estate or gift tax valuation discount.

LLC member/employees are not eligible for non-taxable fringe benefits like health insurance, medical reimbursement, group term insurance, etc.

Members of LLC who actively manage business must pay self-employment tax on distributive share of LLC income. *Prop. Reg. Sec. 1.1402(a)-18(a)* and *Priv. Ltr. Rul. 9432018*.

Possibility that IRS might argue that member has retained complete control over LLC assets and therefore LLC assets would be included in member's estate.

Conversion of "C" or "S" corporation to a LLC where there are appreciated assets may cause taxable gain.

What are the estate planning features of a limited liability company?

LLCs receive a *Code Sec. 1014* step-up in basis (both "inside" and "outside" basis) when member dies. Subchapter "S" owners get only "outside" basis step-up in basis upon death.

LLCs can distribute appreciated property to members without gain (unlike "S" corporation).

LLCs provide flexibility since members can be of different classes and different entities (such as grantor trusts). With an "S" corporation, using a grantor trust can result in phantom income and upon grantor's death, the eligibility for "S" status is limited.

LLCs allow use of "estate freeze" techniques previously utilized prior to enactment of *Code Sec. 2036(b)* (anti-Byrum provisions). One class of members could be "voting" members of LLC and another class could be "non-voting".

Complex trusts could be LLC members.

"S" corporation could form LLC.

"C" corporation could form LLC.

Active participation by LLC member creates either active income or loss to member thereby escaping passive loss rules of *Code Sec. 469*.

LLCs create possible discounts in valuation of LLC property for estate tax purposes (lack of marketability, minority discounts).

LLCs could be used as an alternative to an irrevocable life insurance trust.

Transfer of real property to LLC avoid ancillary probate of the realty.

Member's interest is subject only to creditor's "charging order" (same as limited partner).

LLC provides a mechanism for control of assets by the older generation while increasing the younger generation's ownership and participation in a family business.

Asset protection provided to members for business generated liability.

Foreign ownership permitted.

LLC COMPARISON CHART

	LLC	C CORP	S CORP	GENERAL PARTNER-SHIP	LTD PARTNERSHIP
How is income taxed?	As partnership (unless "S" or "C" corporation elected and single member LLC is Schedule C)	At corporate level and shareholder level	Typically taxed at shareholder level	Not taxed at entity level; pass through to partners	Not taxed at entity level; pass through to partners
What are tax consequences of distribution?	No gain to members	Gain recognized at corporate level	Gain recognized	No gain to partners	No gain to partners
Income taxed by Florida	No	Yes	No	No	No
Liability to owners	Limited	Limited	Limited	Unlimited	General partners, unlimited; Limited partner, limited
May owners freely transfer interests?	No	Yes	Yes	By agreement only	By agreement only
Terms of Existence?	Term of Years of perpetual	Perpetual	Perpetual	Indefinite	Indefinite
How Managed?	Members or special managers	Board of Directors	Board of Directors	All partners	General Partners
Who can be owners?	Unlimited. Any person of entity	Unlimited. Any person of entity	75 max. Only individual subject to exception	Unlimited	Unlimited
What is the effect on owners's tax basis when entity increase liabilities?	Basis increased by share of liability	None	None	Basis increased by share of liability	Basis increased by share of liability

Chapter IV
GRATs, GRUTs & QPRTs – A Planning Overview

What has been the impact of the 2001 Tax Act on estate planning strategies?

The *Economic Growth and Tax Relief Reconciliation Act ("EGTRRA") of 2001* (the "2001 Tax Act" or "Act") has affected transfer tax and estate planning strategies. The 2001 Tax Act is a significant and controversial piece of tax legislation. Whether the Act will survive the current round of legislative warfare is unknown. Congress is in the throes of passing a "new" tax act, therefore the ultimate impact of The 2001 Tax Act is speculative since the "new" tax act may have an impact on the Act's application.

The effect of the 2001 Tax Act on estate planning is very complicated and unsure due to the fact that most of the substantial estate or gift tax benefits provided by the Act are postponed for several years and the Act contains a "sunset" provision that will automatically reinstate the estate tax in the year 2011 unless Congress enacts new legislation. Therefore, it is unclear whether, in fact, Congress will allow the estate tax to be repealed as is scheduled in the 2001 Tax Act.

In any event, we should be aware of the differences between the key aspects of the new estate and gift tax scheme of taxation under the 2001 Tax Act and our prior law, i.e. pre-2002 law. First of all, the prior law provides that estate tax rates range from 37% to 55% with an additional 5% assessment on asset values between $10 million and $17 million. The new law, which is subject to the automatic reinstatement of the present law due to the "sunset" provision referenced above, provides that in the year 2002 the top tax rate is 50%. In the year 2003 through 2006, the top rate drops by 1% per year. For 2007 through 2009, the top rate is set at 45%. In the year 2010, the estate tax is repealed but the gift tax remains in place.

Pre-2002 law provided that the unified credit equivalent or estate tax exemption, i.e. the amount of estate assets that can pass free of estate tax to non-spousal recipients, would increase as follows:

-for the year 2001, the exemption is $675,000 per person;
-for the years 2002 and 2003, the exemption is $700,000 per person;
-for the year 2004, the exemption is $850,000 per person;
-for the year 2005, the exemption is $950,000 per person;
-for the year 2006 and thereafter, the exemption is $1,000,000.

The Act provides that the exemption will be $1,000,000 for the years 2002 and 2003, $1.5 million for the years 2004 and 2005, $2 million for the years 2006 through 2008, $3.5 million for the year 2009 and then, unless the estate tax law is to "sunset", the estate tax will be "automatically" repealed in the year 2010. Below is a chart of the new estate, GST and gift tax rates and exemption amounts created by the Act.

Pre-2002 law also provided that transfers by gift or at death to the surviving spouse are subject to an unlimited marital deduction and thus not taxed. The Act does not change the marital deduction.

Under the pre-2002 law, the adjusted tax basis for property passing from a decedent's estate generally benefits from a stepped-up basis equal to the fair market value of the asset as of the date of the decedent's death. The Act, after the year 2009, changes this rule and imposes a carryover basis for inherited assets except for the fact that the estate can allocate up to $1.3 million in increase in basis to estate assets and an additional $3 million if the property passes to a surviving spouse.

The 2001 Tax Act ("Act")
Chart of Unified Credit Equivalent or
Exemption and Estate, GST and Gift Tax Rates

	ESTATE & GST TAXES		**GIFT TAXES**	
Year	Unified Credit Equivalent (Exempt Amount)	Highest Tax Rate	Exempt Amount	Highest Tax Rate
2002	$1 million	50%	$1 million	50%
2003	$1 million	49%	$1 million	49%
2004	$1.5 million	48%	$1 million	48%
2005	$1.5 million	47%	$1 million	47%
2006	$2 million	46%	$1 million	46%
2007	$2 million	45%	$1 million	45%
2008	$2 million	45%	$1 million	45%
2009	$3.5 million	45%	$1 million	45%
2010	Estate and GST Taxes repealed (subject to sunset provision of Act)	Estate and GST Taxes repealed (subject to sunset provision of Act)	$1 million	Top individual income tax rate

The pre-2002 law provided and permitted a credit against the federal estate tax liability for amounts paid for the state death taxes. The state death tax credit is reduced incrementally in the Act by 25% in the year 2002, by 50% in the year 2003, by 75% in the year 2004, and is repealed in the year 2005 when it is then replaced by deduction.

Under the pre-2002 law, there was a gift tax annual exclusion of $10,000 (in 2005 the annual exclusion is $11,000) for gifts made to a donee on a per recipient basis each calendar year. There was an annual exclusion of $20,000 (in 2005 the combined exclusion is $22,000) if the spouse splits the gift with a donor spouse. Gifts in excess of the annual exclusion reduce the unified credit of the donor and are eventually taxed at the same rate within the estate. The Act provides that the annual exclusion rules are retained, but a lifetime gift tax exemption is capped at $1,000,000 in 2002, and after 2010, the gift tax remains with the rate set at the highest individual income tax rate.

The pre-2002 law provided for a generation skipping transfer tax that imposed a 55% transfer tax on amounts in excess of $1.06 million per person for transfers made to a beneficiary two or more generations below that of the transferor. The Act provides that the generation skipping tax exemption and rate to be generally parallel to the changing estate credit equivalent and tax rate.

It should also be kept in mind that a good portion of estate planning has nothing to do with estate and gift taxation, ex. asset protection planning, avoidance of probate, business continuation planning, asset management for disabled persons, etc.. Estate planning inherently involves selecting strategies and mechanisms to accomplish transfer of assets to family members in a prudent and well-managed manner. Surviving spouses, children and other individuals will still require different types of trusts for asset management and asset protection purposes. Tax law changes do not erase the need for different types of trusts that accomplish varied private or charitable objectives.

The 2001 Tax Act raises a variety of immediate tax issues within an estate planning context that should be immediately addressed. For example, many people use so-called “credit shelter” trusts in their revocable living trust documents. Under the typical “credit shelter” trust plan format, an amount equal to the unified credit equivalent will be carved out at the death of the first spouse to die and placed in trust for the benefit of the surviving spouse and/or lineal heirs. The objective is to use the unified credit equivalent or exemption of the first spouse to die regardless of the order of death, and therefore forever exempt the unused unified credit equivalent amount from estate tax in the estate of either spouse. In essence, spouses can preserve and exempt from estate tax estate assets that equal the amount of each spouse’s unified credit equivalent by the use of a credit shelter trust plan, usually referred to as a “revocable A/B trust” or “living trust”. If you have such an estate plan, it should be reviewed due to the fact that the scheduled increases in the unified credit might place too many estate assets in the "credit shelter" trust.

The 2001 Tax Act may somewhat alter the implementation of time-honored estate and gift tax minimization strategies, but the Act does not eliminate the use of these strategies. In fact, due to the increase in the available unified credit equivalent amount, there are new planning opportunities created when utilizing GRATs, GRUTs and QPRTs. GRATs, GRUTs and QPRTs leverage the use of the unified credit and with more such unified credit available, these planning techniques become more advantageous. The rest of this article will specifically address and analyze the use, structure and beneficial aspects of GRATs, GRUT and QPRTs.

What are GRATs and GRUTs?

There are a particular species of grantor trusts known as grantor retained annuity trusts (GRATs) and grantor retained unitrusts (GRUTs) that are specifically authorized by *Internal Revenue Service Code ("Code") Sec. 2702* and are designed to generate a legally permissible "freeze" of the taxable value of property that is transferred to such trusts. The phrase "estate tax freeze" basically means that the future appreciation value of property transferred to such a trust will escape gift or estate taxation (a/k/a transfer taxes). During the 1970s and 1980s, estate planners used a variety of split interest trusts such as grantor retained income trusts (GRITs) and other legal arrangements involving gifts with retained interests in order to "freeze" the value of assets expected to appreciate in the future and to give away that anticipated appreciation free of any gift or estate tax. In order to create a disincentive for the use of such planning techniques, Congress passed a variety of special valuation rules designed to defeat or limit "estate tax freezes". Ultimately, Congress passed *Chapter 14 to the Internal Revenue Code* in 1990 that implemented *Code Sections 2701 through 2704*. These Code sections created new rules governing split interest trusts and other estate freezing planning strategies. Thus, GRATs and GRUTs were "born".

GRATs and GRUTs are sometimes referred to as intentionally income tax defective grantor trusts ("IDGT) because such trusts are designed to have the grantor taxed as the owner of the trust corpus for income tax purposes as per *Code Sections 671-679*. The objective in a GRAT or GRUT is to draft a trust instrument that is "income tax defective" to the grantor, yet make the trust effective for gift tax and estate tax purposes.

Chapter 14 approaches the estate tax freeze problem as essentially a gift tax valuation issue. Transfers of any interest by a grantor to a trust whereby the grantor retains an interest therein is specifically governed by *Code Section 2702.*

Code Section 2702 says that the grantor's retained interest in such a trust will have a fair market value for estate and gift tax valuation purposes only if it is a "qualified interest". *Code Section 2702(a)(2)(B)* provides that there are two general types of "qualified interest" trusts, to-wit: A grantor retained annuity trust (GRAT) and a grantor retained unitrust (GRUT). Essentially, a grantor retained annuity trust (GRAT) constitutes a gift of a future remainder interest in the property that is placed within an irrevocable trust whereby the grantor retains the right to receive a fixed amount, payable at least annually, for a term of years or for the life of the grantor. *Code Section 2702(b)(1); Reg. Sec. 27.2702-3(b).* A grantor retained unitrust (GRUT) is structured in a similar way except that the grantor retains the right to receive an annuity equal to a fixed percentage of the fair market value of the trust property that is determined on an annual basis. *Code Sec. 2702(b)(2); Reg. Sec. 25.2702-3(c).*

In the creation of a GRAT or GRUT, the grantor is considered to have made a completed gift of the remainder interest in the trust that would come to fruition after the expiration of the trust term. As a result, a transfer of assets to a GRAT or GRUT is a taxable gift only to the extent of the value of the remainder interest in the trust assets. The annuity interest of the grantor is valued based upon the present value of the annuity. *Code Sec. 2702(a)(2)(B); Reg. Sec. 25.2702-2(b)(2); Tables B and S in IRS Publication 1457; Reg. Sec. 20.2031-7.*

The regulations require GRATs and GRUTs to have the following mutually common characteristics in order to be "qualified interest" trusts under *Code Sec. 2702*:

1. GRATs and GRUTs must function as such from the first day of trust's creation.

2. GRAT and GRUT structures cannot be mixed with one another. *Reg. Sec. 25.2702-3(d)(1).*

3. GRATs or GRUTs cannot distribute principal or income to anyone during the trust term other than the designated annuitant. *Reg. Sec. 25.2705-3(d)(2).*

4. GRATs or GRUTs must provide for a fixed term retained annuity interest to the grantor. The term can be for a term of years or for the life of the annuitant. *Reg. Sec. 25.2702-3(d)(3). CAVEAT:* There is an estate tax inclusion issue and problem if a life term is chosen by the grantor. The IRS will claim a 100% inclusion of trust assets upon grantor's death!

5. A GRAT or GRUT must prohibit the commutation of the interest of the grantor as annuitant. *Reg. Sec. 25.2702-3(d)(4).*

In addition to the above requirements, GRATs must also comply with the following rules:

1. The annuity in a GRAT must be an irrevocable right to receive a fixed amount payable at least once a year or in more often installments during the year, i.e., quarterly or monthly. *Reg. Sec. 25.2702-3(b)(1).* Failure to distribute the annuity will result in disqualification of the GRAT. The annuity amount can be either a fixed dollar amount or expressed as a percentage of the initial fair market value of the assets used to fund the GRAT.

2. The GRAT must contain a provision that requires the trustee to make compensating payments to the annuitant if there is an incorrect valuation made of the initial trust assets.

3. The GRAT must contain a provision that requires the adjustment of the annuity in the event of a short taxable year or in the last year of the trust. *Reg. Sec. 25.2702-3(b)(3).*

4. The GRAT must prohibit additional contributions to the trust. *Reg. Sec. 25.2702-3(b)(4).*

GRUTs must comply with the following rules:

1. A qualified unitrust interest in a GRUT must constitute an irrevocable right to receive a fixed percentage of the annual value of the trust once a year (or more frequent intervals). *Reg. Sec. 25.2702-3(c)(1).*

2. The trustee of a GRUT must make compensating payments to the annuitant where incorrect valuation of the trust asset have occurred.

3. A GRUT must require the unitrust to be adjusted in the event of short taxable years or in the year the GRUT ends.

In either a GRAT or GRUT, the annuity or unitrust amount can be structured to change each year to the extent that the variance in any given year is not more than 20% of the preceding year's annuity or unitrust amount. *Reg. Sections 25.2702-3(b)(1)(ii), 25.2702-3(c)(1)(ii), 25.2702.31(e), 25.2702-3(e)(Ex. 5), Priv. Ltr. Rul. 9451056.* There is no apparent restriction on the amount of planned decrease so long as the annuity or unitrust amount is not less than 5% per annum.

Other than GRATs and GRUTs, there is a third type of trust, a qualified personal residence trust ("QPRT"), that is also considered "qualified interest" trust pursuant to *Code Sec.2702.* A QPRT is a split interest trust that is classified as a grantor retained income trust ("GRIT"). A QPRT is an irrevocable trust whereby a grantor conveys either a personal residence or vacation residence into the trust and the grantor retains the right to exclusively use the trust property for a specified period of years. The QPRT will be discussed further hereinbelow.

What is a QPRT?

Another type or species of "qualified interest" trust that is authorized by the regulations under *Code Sec. 2702* is the qualified personal residence trust (QPRT). *Reg. Sec. 25.2702-5(c).* A QPRT is designed to specifically hold title to a homestead residence and a vacation residence. *Reg. Sec. 25.2702-5(c)(5).* A QPRT can be created to first hold title to a homestead residence, thereafter a second QPRT can be created to hold title to a secondary or "vacation" residence. In a QPRT, title to qualifying property is transferred to an irrevocable trust for a specific term of years. This term of years can be based upon the expected mortality of the grantor or some other shorter term. The trustee of the QPRT may be the grantor who manages the trust assets. Usually, the grantor and spouse of the QPRT are the term beneficiaries of the trust. At the expiration of the trust term, distribution of the trust assets are made as designated in the QPRT instrument. After the expiration of the trust term, the value of the QPRT property is excluded from the grantor's estate. The entire value of the QPRT property, i.e., the fair market value of the QPRT property as of the date of the grantor's death is included in the gross estate of the grantor should the grantor die during the QPRT term. This risk of inclusion destroys the estate tax savings possibilities for the QPRT, but such risk can be mitigated through the purchase of life insurance on the life of the grantor. The grantor can retain the homestead exemption and the other tax attributes of a homestead residence. *Robbins v. Welbaum, 664 So.2d 1 (Fla. 3d DCA 1995).*

In a manner similar to a GRAT or GRUT, a QPRT is an irrevocable trust whereby the grantor is making a completed gift of a future interest in the trust property while retaining an exclusive use of the property as the term beneficiary of the trust. As is the case with a GRAT or GRUT, the higher the value of the retained interest to the grantor, the lower the value of the gift is of the remainder interest for gift tax purposes. A QPRT, like a GRAT or GRUT, has the effect of leveraging the grantor's unified credit and generating estate tax savings. In addition, like a GRAT or GRUT, the QPRT may be a limited asset protected environment as against Florida state law future potential creditors and creates a non-probate disposition of the trust property in the event of death during the trust term. The QPRT has other beneficial features, such as the option that can be created within a QPRT that would allow the grantor to sell the homestead residence at grantor's discretion and convert some or all of the proceeds of the sale into a GRAT and thus generate an additional cash flow to the grantor. *Reg. Sec. 25.2702-5(c)(8)(I)(B).*

The IRS has a proposed regulation (*Reg. Sec. 25.2702-5*) that requires the QPRT instrument to include a prohibition that the grantor of the QPRT shall not be allowed to reacquire or repurchase the QPRT residence from the QPRT.

In the case referenced above, Robbins v. Welbaum, supra, it was held that the grantor of a QPRT retains Florida homestead property tax benefits. However, this case did not address the issue of whether a QPRT property retains the benefit of being considered a constitutionally exempt "homestead" property for purposes of protection against attack by a future creditor.

The IRS has permitted so-called "appurtenant structures" and "adjacent land" to be considered part of the personal residence for QPRT purposes. *Priv. Ltr. Rul. 200112018.* The *Code Sec. 2702* regulations do permit a second kind of trust that can hold title to personal residences that is called a "personal residence trust" (PRT). However a PRT is much less useful than a QPRT due to the restrictions and lack of flexibility.

What does "qualified interest" mean and why is the qualification of a trust as a GRAT or GRUT important?

When a grantor of a split-interest trust retains an interest in the trust, e.g., an annuity interest, and makes a present gift of a future remainder interest by virtue of the trust to a family member, e.g., grantor's spouse, ancestor of the grantor or grantor's spouse, or the spouse of any such ancestor, then *Code Sec. 2702(a)* causes the value of the grantor's retained interest to be zero for purposes of calculating the value of the gift. However, if the grantor's retained interest is a "qualified interest" pursuant to *Code Sec. 2702(b),* then the value of the grantor's retained interest shall be appropriately valued and subtracted from the total initial value of the trust corpus for purposes of ascertaining the gift tax value of the trust's remainder interest. A "qualified interest" refers to a qualified annuity interest in a GRAT and a qualified unitrust interest in a GRUT. *Reg. Sec. 25.2702-2(a)(5).*

To be a "qualified annuity interest" in a GRAT, all of the requirements of *Reg. Sec. 25.2702-3(b)* must be met while a "qualified unitrust interest" in a GRUT must meet the requirements of *Reg. Sec. 25.2702-3(c).* These requirements have been discussed above.

Generally, what are the beneficial effects of using GRATs, GRUTs and QPRTs?

By properly structuring GRATs, GRUTs or a QPRT, the problems of under-utilization of your unified credit, estate appreciation and estate liquidity problems can be solved to a great extent. The problems of reducing or eliminating probate and estate administration expenses, asset protection and financial management for you and your lineal heirs can also be addressed by the use of GRATs, GRUTs and QPRTs.

Why is it desirable for a GRAT, GRUT or QPRT to be considered a grantor trust for income tax purposes pursuant to *Code Sections 671-679*?

Transactions between the grantor and the grantor trust do not cause recognition of gain or loss to the grantor based upon *Rev. Rul. 85-13, 1985-1 CB 184*, i.e., funding the trust with appreciated property, in-kind distributions to the grantor/beneficiary to satisfy the annuity payment, grantor's exchange of equal valued property to the trust.

In a QPRT, the grantor could deduct mortgage interest and property taxes paid on QPRT property (*Priv.Ltr.Rul. 9448035*), grantor could take advantage of the former *Code Sec. 121* exclusion on the profit from the sale of the residence by the QPRT (*Rev. Rul. 85-45, 1985-1 CB 183; Priv.Ltr.Rul. 9118017*), grantor could take advantage of deferral of gain under *Code Sec. 1034* (*Rev. Rul. 66-159, 1966-1 CB 162; Priv.Ltr.Rul. 9026036*), and, as previously mentioned, the grantor can claim the homestead exemption for property tax purposes, <u>Robbins v. Welbaum</u> *case*, supra.

How does someone creating a GRAT, GRUT or QPRT assure that the grantor shall be treated as the owner of the trust corpus for income tax purposes?

If a grantor is deemed the owner of the trust corpus, all items of income, deductions, credits and losses pass through to the grantor's individual tax return. *Code Sec. 671*. In order to properly structure the trust to become "intentionally income tax defective", the trust should give the grantor one or more of those powers referred to in *Code Sec. 673-679*. Some common powers given to a grantor in order to create the desired scheme of taxation (***CAVEAT:*** Not all these powers are appropriate for use in a GRAT, GRUT or QPRT):

1. Grantor retains the owner in a non-fiduciary capacity, without approval or consent of any trust fiduciary, to reacquire any part of the trust corpus by substituting by exchange property of equal value. *Code Sec. 675(4)(c); Priv.Ltr.Rul. 9446008, 9403020, 9352017, 9247024.* A grantor's spouse may also hold such a power. If a grantor is acting as trustee, he or she cannot exercise the power of substitute assets because of fiduciary status. *Reg. Sec. 1.675-1(b)(4). See, Reg. Sec. 1.675-1(b)(4)(iii),* as to facts and circumstances that indicate whether grantor holds such a power in a non-fiduciary capacity. This type of power is effective as substituting a low basis trust asset with a high basis asset.

2. Inclusion of a contingent reversion provision to grantor's estate (or to grantor's spouse) that will distribute that portion of the trust corpus that is includ-

ed in the grantor's gross estate if the grantor dies during the trust term. *Code Sec. 673.* A reversionary interest in both income and principal causes grantor to be treated as the owner of the entire trust under *Code Sec. 673(a). Priv. Ltr. Rul. 9519029.*

3. In the case of a GRAT, the fact that the annuity is paid from trust income, and if insufficient from trust principal, causes the GRAT to be taxed under *Code Sec. 677(a).*

4. Include a power to lend trust assets to the grantor without adequate security. *Code Sec. 675(2).*

5. Include a power to have related or subordinate trustees to sprinkle income or principal among beneficiaries unlimited by a reasonably ascertainable standard. *Code Sec. 674(c).*

6. Give a non-adverse party (other than the grantor) the power to enlarge the class of remaindermen. *Code Sec. 674(a).*

When will using a GRAT make the most amount of sense for a client?

The best reasons for using a GRAT are:

1. The grantor has high basis, income-producing liquid assets that shall be used to fund the trust.

2. GRAT assets will grow in excess of applicable *Code Section 7520* rate during retained annuity term and annuity rate is less than the growth rate.

3. The grantor has unused unified gift that he or she wishes to leverage.

4. The grantor can afford to use a trust term for years that grantor will likely survive.

5. The grantor has a taxable estate and wishes to minimize or eliminate transfer taxes on the disposition of assets to other persons.

How do you choose between a GRAT or GRUT?

First of all, if maximized estate tax savings are most important, the GRAT is the best planning choice. If the GRAT corpus grows in excess of the *Code Sec. 7520* rate, estate tax savings are enhanced in comparison to a GRUT. A GRAT is simpler and cheaper to administer since a GRUT requires annual valuation of its assets and a GRAT only requires an initial valuation of trust assets.

Regardless of whether a GRAT or GRUT is used, the grantor should fund either trust with assets that shall generate enough income to pay the required annuity and shall hopefully appreciate at a rate in excess of the *Code Sec. 7520* rate. Otherwise, the use of either type of trust shall be futile and non-productive for purposes of estate tax savings. Also, in order to assure complete exclusion of the trust corpus from estate taxation, the trust term should be a period of time that the grantor shall be reasonably expected to survive.

What are the estate planning advantages of the GRATs and GRUTs?

A GRAT or GRUT offers the following potential estate planning advantages:

1. Since a GRAT or GRUT is considered an immediate gift of the remainder interest in the trust assets, any future appreciation of those assets inures to the benefit of the designated remainderman to the trust assets and are therefore removed from additional estate taxation upon the death of the grantor, assuming the grantor survives the trust term. In this way, a GRAT or GRUT creates an "estate tax freeze" that generates tangible estate tax savings. This aspect of using a GRAT or GRUT is only relevant when the grantor has a taxable estate at death and the grantor survives the trust term.

2. In a GRAT or GRUT, the grantor must retain an annuity cash flow interest from the trust in an amount not to be less than 5%. Said annuity can be scheduled to automatically increase at a rate not to exceed 20% per year or decrease to an annuity rate not less than 5%. If the trust assets generate a return that exceeds the annuity percentage, the additional income will be accumulated within the trust for the benefit of the remainderman without additional gift tax liability.

3. From an estate tax savings standpoint, the only way to guarantee 100% exclusion of the value of the trust assets from being included in the taxable estate of the grantor, the grantor must survive a trust term that is scheduled for a term of years.

4. Since a GRAT or GRUT is specifically approved as a "qualified interest" under Chapter 14, the remainder interest that is considered a gift is valued under traditional gift tax rules and is not subject to the special gift tax valuation rules of

Chapter 14 of the Code. When the trust is created, a gift tax return (Form 709) is filed with the Internal Revenue Service in order to report the taxable gift.

5. Since a GRAT or GRUT is an irrevocable trust that cannot be commuted, such a trust, to the extent of trust corpus, has limited asset protection qualities for the benefit of the grantor so long as the grantor does not have any present or past creditors at the time of creation of the trust so that fraudulent transfer laws are not violated. Since a GRAT or GRUT is a "self-settled" trust, it appears under Florida law that creditors of the grantor can seize the annuity or unitrust amount paid. cf. *In re Jane McLean Brown, 303 F.3d 1261 (11th Cir. 2002).*

6. GRAT or GRUT assets are disposed of at the end of the trust term in a non-probate fashion which saves the estate administration costs to the grantor's estate. Such trusts allow specific and certain distribution of trust assets upon expiration of the trust term.

7. A GRAT or GRUT can be domiciled in a foreign situs so long as there is compliance with local law in terms of the creation and administration of the trust. This strategy affords additional asset protection and provides other tax planning options. A grantor can avoid the "self-settled" trust problem referenced above by use of a foreign situs GRAT.

8. A GRAT or GRUT is income tax neutral to the grantor. The grantor of a GRAT or GRUT is deemed to be the owner of the trust corpus for income tax purposes and must include into individual income all taxable income generated by the trust each taxable year. If ever the trust generates a tax liability that exceeds annuity paid to the grantor, through a reimbursement provision in the trust, the GRAT or GRUT may reimburse the grantor for such excess tax liability so that the grantor will not be out-of-pocket to pay any income tax liability generated by the trust. If the grantor is trustee, there should be no tax reimbursement provision in the trust. The trust must file a Form 1041 if a third party acts as trustee. If the grantor also serves as trustee, all trust income is reported on grantor's Form 1040 and no form 1041 is required. *Reg. Sec. 1.671-4(b).* No federal identification number is necessary for the trust if the grantor is trustee or co-trustee.

9. The grantor, by law, is the only recipient of the trust annuity during the trust term. If trust income is less than the annuity payment required, then trust principal is paid to the grantor in order to make up the difference. Promissory notes cannot be used to satisfy the annuity obligation.

10. The grantor may act as trustee or grantor may appoint any qualified person or entity as trustee.

11. A GRAT or GRUT may be scheduled to have either a term of years that

does not exceed the actuarial mortality of the grantor, or a term for the life of the grantor (***CAVEAT***: IRS will take position that all trust assets are includible in grantor's estate if grantor dies during trust term).

12. The grantor, as trustee, can manage and control GRAT or GRUT assets as provided by law for the term of the trust.

13. The calculated value of the gift of the remainder interest in the GRAT or GRUT can be increased or decreased as a tax planning strategy depending upon a variety of variables, i.e., the age of grantor, the term of the trust, the annuity or unitrust amount, the *Code Sec. 7520* rate at the time of creation of the trust, the scheduled rate of increase in the annuity amount. In order to lower the gift tax value of the remainder interest, the following relationships hold true:

a. The younger the age of the grantor, the smaller the gift.
b. The longer the term of the trust, the smaller the gift.
c. The greater the annuity amount, the smaller the gift.
d. The lower the *Code Sec. 7520* rate, the smaller the gift.
e. If there is a scheduled rate of increase in the annuity amount, the smaller the gift.

14. If a grantor dies during the term of a GRAT or GRUT, whatever portion of the unified credit the grantor used at the time the trust was created is restored and is used again as a credit against the grantor's estate taxes in the grantor's final Form 706. *Code Sec. 2001(b).*

15. The GRAT or GRUT allows for the leveraged use of the grantor's unified credit and therefore results in a far superior transfer tax consequence to the grantor making an outright gift of assets in the amount of grantor's unified credit (or any portion thereof). The leverage occurs because the grantor is making a gift of a future interest that is actuarially valued based upon how long the remaindermen of the trust must wait to receive his or her "gift" of the remaining trust corpus. The longer the wait, the lower the amount of the gift. In the interim, the grantor gets to receive the annuity, thus the grantor "gets his or her cake and gets to eat it too". An additional leveraging advantage is generated when discounted value entities, for example, "S" corporations, limited partnerships, limited liability companies, are used to fund the GRAT and GRUT.

16. There is no age limitation in using a GRAT or GRUT as far as the grantor is concerned. Obviously, the older the grantor, the less gift tax leverage will occur.

What are the disadvantages of using a GRAT or GRUT?

There are several potential disadvantages or issues of concern that must be considered before creating a GRAT or GRUT:

1. A GRAT or a GRUT is subject to the grantor trust rules of *Internal Revenue Code Sections 671-679* for income tax purposes. Accordingly, all income tax consequences generated by the GRAT or GRUT are passed through to the grantor who is responsible for reporting and paying for any taxable income generated by the trust regardless of the annuity payment. The GRAT or GRUT does not alter the individual income tax consequences of the grantor.

2. Once you transfer assets to create a GRAT, the grantor cannot provide additional funding to that GRAT in the future. GRUT assets need to be appraised annually which typically eliminates real estate and other assets that are difficult to value as GRUT asset candidates.

3. As mentioned above, if the grantor retains a lifetime annuity interest in the GRAT or GRUT or dies during the term of the trust, there will usually be some (or all) inclusion of the value of the original trust assets in the grantor's estate at the time of death due to *Code Sec. 2036*. The inclusion calculation is obviously affected by the amount of the annuity dictated by the grantor at the time of death, the fluctuation in the Section 7520 interest rate and other factors. See, *Rev. Rul. 82-105, 1982-1C.B. 133; Rev. Rul. 76-723, 1976-2 C.B. 268; Estate of Becklenberg, 31 TC 402, rev'd 273 F.2d 297.* ***CAVEAT:*** The IRS may include the entire trust corpus into grantor's estate per *Code Sec. 2039*, in addition to *Code Sec. 2036* rationale (see discussion below).

4. Neither the grantor nor the beneficiary of a GRAT or GRUT should pledge or sell trust assets for his or her personal benefit outside of the trust.

5. Since the gift portion of the GRAT or GRUT is a future remainder interest, no part of any taxable remainder interest can qualify for the $11,000 per year, per person gift tax annual exclusion.

6. A GRAT or GRUT is considered a separate and distinct legal entity that requires a formal trust agreement that complies with *Code Section 2702* and the applicable regulations. All taxable income must be properly reported on a yearly basis. A Form 709 (Federal Gift Tax Return) must be filed to record the value of gift made by virtue of creation of the trust, i.e., the present value of the remainder interest of the trust.

7. Typically, only income producing assets are good asset candidates for a GRAT or GRUT since the annuity must be paid every year from the trust to the grantor.

8. Since a GRAT or GRUT is an irrevocable trust, the ultimate beneficiaries at

the death of the grantor lose a stepped-up basis under Code Sec. 1014 on trust assets distributed. Therefore, high basis assets are the best candidates to be used for funding the trust.

9. The IRS has previously in two private letter rulings (*Priv. Ltr. Ruls. 9451056, 9345035*) taken the position that if the grantor dies during the term of the trust that *Code Sec. 2039* would require inclusion of the entire value of the trust property due to the grantor's retention of an annuity interest until death. The opposing argument to the above position is that *Code Sec. 2039* does not apply to a GRAT or GRUT and that the calculation required by *Rev. Rul. 82-105* would apply instead for estate tax inclusion and valuation purposes.

10. The grantor must bear the costs of implementing the trust, including attorney's fees, accountant's fees, appraisal fees, trustee fees, property re-titling costs and other related expenses.

11. If trust income is insufficient to pay the annuity amount, trust corpus must be used to pay the annuity which shall deplete the trust value and reduce the estate tax savings. If trust corpus growth is insufficient in being less than the *Code Sec. 7520* rate which was assumed for the trust, the estate tax savings will also be lost.

What are grantor retained income trusts (GRITs)?

Prior to the enactment of Chapter 14 in 1990, senior generation family members would transfer property to an irrevocable trust and then retain an income interest for a specified term. These types of trusts were known as grantor retained income trusts (GRITs). *Code Sec. 2702* greatly reduced the use of GRITs. GRITs are now used for family members only for personal residences (QPRT) and for non-income producing tangible personal property. GRITs can still be used for non-family members. Family members include transferor's spouse; any ancestor or descendant of transferor or spouse; any sibling of transferor; and the spouse of any ancestor, descendant or sibling. Family members <u>do not</u> include descendants of siblings, i.e., nieces and nephews. *Code Sec. 2702(e), 2704(c)(2).*

Can paintings, sculptures, objects of art, collectible antique automobiles and other items of tangible personal property be used to fund a grantor trust?

Yes. *Code Sec. 2702(c)(4)* provides an exception to the *Code Sec. 2702* gift tax valuation rules for the transfer of a term interest in tangible non-depreciable property. *Reg. Sec. 25.2702-2(c)(2).*

In creating a GRAT, can the qualified annuity interest be set up so that the value of the annuity equals the value of assets used to fund the GRAT thus eliminating the gift tax value of the remainder interest in the GRAT, i.e., is it possible to "zero out" a gift to a GRAT?

The IRS has argued the position, pursuant to *Reg. Sec. 25.2702-3(e), Ex. 5* and Rev. *Rul. 77-454, 1977-2 C.B. 351,* that a GRAT cannot be "zeroed out". Prop. Reg. Sec. 1.7520-3(b)(2)(I). However, on December 22, 2000, the U.S. Tax Court held in a case captioned *Walton v. Commissioner, 115 T.C. No. 41,* that Reg. Sec. *25.2702-3(e), Ex. 5*, was invalid thus dealing a fatal blow to the IRS argument and position vis-a-vis "zeroed out GRATs".

If a GRAT does not have sufficient cash to pay to the grantor the required annuity, what happens?

There are two alternatives for the trustee: the trustee can distribute trust assets in kind to satisfy the annuity; or the trustee can borrow money on trust assets and then distribute loan proceeds to satisfy the annuity. If a trustee seeks to satisfy the annuity amount with a note, the IRS will say the trust is not a qualified interest trust. *TAM 9717008.* In proposed regulations, the IRS has prohibited the effective use of notes or other debt instruments by a GRAT trustee in satisfaction of the GRAT annuity obligation. *Prop. Reg. Sec. 25.2702-3(b)(1)(I); Prop. Reg. Sec. 25.2702-3(c)(1)(I); Prop. Reg. Sec. 25-2703-3(d)(5).*

In a GRAT, may the grantor borrow from the trust without adequate security?

Yes.

In a GRAT, may the grantor reacquire trust property by substituting other property of equal value?

Yes. *Code Sec. 675(4)(c).*

May a GRAT own Subchapter "S" stock?

Yes. *Code Sec. 1361(c)(2)(A).*

May a GRAT own partnership and limited liability company interests?

Yes.

How do you maximize the estate freeze value of a GRAT?

Choose a trust term that the grantor shall likely survive. In that scenario, if the return on the trust property exceeds the *Code Sec. 7520* rate, then the GRAT will produce estate tax savings.

Can a GRAT be used to generate any freezing of values for generation skipping tax (GST) purposes?

No. *Code Sec. 2702* does not apply to GSTs. When a GRAT terminates, the entire value of the trust property is counted for GST purposes.

What happens if the GRAT generates taxable income in a given year that exceeds the cash flow provided by the annuity to the grantor and then grantor must pay a tax in excess of the annuity amount?

The trust instrument can provide a tax reimbursement provision that requires the trustee to reimburse the grantor for the tax liability due in excess of the annuity amount. The IRS has apparently required the inclusion of such a tax reimbursement provision in order for the GRAT, GRUT or QPRT to qualify under *Code Sec. 2702. Priv. Ltr. Rul. 9519029, 950204021, 9444033 and 9416009.* However, the IRS subsequently issued *Priv. Ltr. Rul. 9540349* that casts some doubt over the issue of whether such a provision is absolutely required. It is advisable to omit tax reimbursement language if the grantor is trustee of the trust.

Can a GRAT or GRUT be created in a foreign situs?

Yes. A foreign situs GRAT or GRUT can be created that will have the same transfer tax attributes of a domestic trust. From a planning perspective, however, a foreign situs GRAT offers additional advantages to the client that are described below:

1. Enhanced asset protection of liquid assets, i.e., stock, bonds, cash, etc. by using a foreign jurisdiction, the law of the foreign situs is used for purposes of determining creditor rights vis-a-vis trust assets.

2. After the death of the grantor, a properly structured foreign situs trust can be used as a GRAT or GRUT remainderman in order to legally defer or avoid U.S. income taxes to U.S. beneficiaries.

3. Foreign trusts can be used to own interests in foreign corporations that generate non-U.S. source income and thus defer taxation.

4. Foreign trusts can be created in countries that do not have income, estate or gift taxes and have other favorable local law features.

5. Foreign trusts afford additional secrecy and protection from U.S. creditors.

How is a foreign situs GRAT taxed?

Any foreign trust formed by a U.S. grantor that has a U.S. beneficiary is taxed as a grantor trust under *Code Sec. 679.* Therefore, a foreign GRAT is taxed just like a domestic GRAT, i.e., the grantor is taxed on all taxable income earned by the trust. *Code Sections 671-679.* In addition, a foreign situs GRAT may require the filing of other applicable forms, such as Forms 926, 3520, 56, SS-4, 1041, 5471, 4790, 8288, 8288A, 3520A and Treasury Form 90-22.1. A gift tax return (Form 709) must be filed showing the extent of use of the grantor's unified credit in a foreign situs GRAT, just like in a domestic GRAT situation.

Can distributions be made from a GRAT or GRUT to someone other than the annuitant during the term of the qualified annuity interest?

No. *Reg. Sec. 25.2702-3(d)(2).*

How long can the term of a GRAT or GRUT be?

The term must be for life of annuitant, for a specified term of years or for the shorter of those two periods. *Reg. Sec. 25.2702-3(d)(3).*

Can a GRAT, GRUT or QPRT be commuted prior to the expiration of its term?

No. *Priv. Ltr. Rul. 9412036.*

May a grantor act as trustee of a GRAT, GRUT or QPRT?

Yes.

May a GRAT permit the payment of income in excess of the annuity amount to the GRAT annuitant?

Yes. *Reg. Sec. 25.2702-3(b)(1(iii).* If such a term is included, that term shall not affect the valuation of the grantor's qualified annuity interest.

Is there any practical limitation as to how high a qualified annuity interest or qualified unitrust can be set in a GRAT or GRUT?

Yes. If it appears that the annuity paid out of a GRAT or GRUT to a grantor may exhaust the trust corpus before the term of the trust expires, then the value of the grantor's retained annuity interest shall be considered no greater than the present value of the payments receivable until the exhaustion of the trust corpus from which the annuity will be paid. See, *Rev. Rul. 77-454, 1977-2 C.B. 35.* Therefore, the trust annuity should not be set at such a rate as will cause complete consumption of the trust fund prior to the trust's scheduled date of termination.

In a GRAT or GRUT where the term is for the life of the

grantor or where the grantor dies during the trust term, what are the estate tax implications to the grantor's estate?

The IRS has taken the position that if the grantor of a GRAT dies during the trust term, the entire trust corpus is includible in the grantor's estate pursuant to *Code Sec. 2039. Priv. Ltr. Ruls. 9451056, 9345035.* The IRS position is ostensibly based upon the theory that the grantor's gross estate should include the value of the GRAT or GRUT annuity due to the fact that the trust remainderman shall receive the corpus by reason of surviving the grantor under an agreement, i.e., the GRAT or GRUT that paid an annuity to the grantor. *Code Sec. 2039(a).* The proposed drafting solution to this dilemma if the grantor is concerned about the risk imposed by the IRS position should the grantor die during the trust term involves the alteration of the standard trust terms to include language that would provide that the trust have a fixed term based upon the expected life of the grantor and that, in the event the grantor died during the trust term, the remaining annuity or unitrust payments be paid to the grantor's estate or devised to the grantor's spouse. In this way, *Code Sec. 2039* is arguably avoided and the present value of the remaining annuity or unitrust payments would be included in the grantor's estate pursuant to *Code Sec. 2033.*

Most recently, in *TAM 200210009*, the IRS determined that when a grantor of a GRAT dies during the GRAT term while retaining a "sufficient" interest in property transferred to fund a GRAT, a portion of the GRAT corpus is includible in the grantor's estate pursuant to *Code Sec. 2036* and, moreover, the total value of the GRAT corpus was includible in the grantor's estate pursuant to *Code Sec. 2039.* Confusing? Yes, indeed. This inclusion issue remains murky and uncertain. In any event, a review of the facts, the issues, the IRS analysis and conclusion is instructive, if not clearly dispositive of the GRAT inclusion dilemma.

The relevant facts pertaining to *TAM 200210009*, were as follows: Mr. D creates a GRAT wherein he and his daughter (Miss D) are co-trustees for a ten year term with a 15% annuity amount. The GRAT provided if grantor died during the term (which he did in Year 6 of the GRAT), then the remaining annuity payments would be paid to his estate and after the tenth year term expires, all GRAT assets are then distributed to Miss D., et al.

The issue was "to what extent is the corpus of the GRAT includible in the decedent grantor's estate under *Code Secs. 2036 or 2039* of the IRC?" Interestingly enough, the IRS said that under *Code Sec. 2036*, the amount includible in the grantor's estate is determined under *Rev. Rul. 82-105, 1982-1 C.B. 133.* Under *Code Sec. 2039,* the IRS said the entire value of the GRAT was includible in the grantor's estate.

In its analysis under *Code Sec. 2036*, the IRS (and I believe correctly so) concluded that *Rev. Rul. 82-105* is applicable in order to calculate the amount of trust corpus necessary to generate the required annuity which establishes the amount of trust corpus includible.

In its analysis under *Code Sec. 2039*, the IRS (and I believe incorrectly so) concluded that since the annuity payments commenced by reason of the grantor's death would be payable to the grantor's estate and that each beneficiary would have had to survive the grantor in order to receive any GRAT payments, then all GRAT post-death annuity payments trigger the application of *Code Sec. 2039(a)* causing inclusion of the entire GRAT corpus into the grantor's gross estate.

The illogic of the *Code Sec. 2039* position vis-a-vis the *Code Sec. 2036* position is obvious. Shouldn't the amount included in the grantor's estate equal the amount of trust corpus necessary to support and pay-out the required GRAT annuity amount? You would think so, but the IRS apparently disagrees. Without clarifying legislation or case law, this "inclusion issue" remains problematic, contentious and uncertain.

From a practical standpoint in terms of drafting a GRAT in light of the above, it appears prudent to consider the GRAT provisions that utilize the martial deduction should the grantor of the GRAT die during its term survived by a spouse. In terms of drafting the GRAT, the remaining annuity could be paid to his or her estate then he or she could devise the payments to the surviving spouse with an additional provision distributing any non-included GRAT assets to non-spousal beneficiaries. Another variation in drafting would provide for payment of the GRAT remainder to the surviving spouse.

To the extent there is an inclusion of trust corpus in the grantor's estate, the grantor's estate is entitled to receive a credit for that portion of the unified credit that was used when the trust was funded and the estate's adjusted taxable gifts under *Code Sec. 2001(b)* would not include any portion of the trust corpus that is includible in the grantor's gross estate.

A few words of wisdom:

1. In a term GRAT or GRUT, the grantor shall always bear the potential risk of death during the trust term and, in such event, you can expect the IRS to take the position that, notwithstanding the above arguments to the contrary, the full fair market value of the trust assets as of the date of the grantor's death will be included in the grantor's estate and, therefore, expect to fight the inclusion issue upon audit. The only way to guarantee a 100% exclusion scenario is for the grantor to survive the trust term, so wisely choose a reasonably survivable trust term. This goes double for a QPRT since a grantor death during a QPRT term guarantees inclusion of the full value of the QPRT property. For exclusion of QPRT assets to

occur, the grantor must survive the QPRT term.

2. Avoid use of life term GRATs and GRUTs for reasons set forth above.

3. The tax cost of inclusion of trust corpus in the grantor's gross estate can be mitigated by the use of life insurance. In order to hedge against the risk of a grantor death during the GRAT, GRUT or QPRT term, buy adequate life insurance to provide liquidity to the estate to take care adverse estate tax consequences caused by such an event. Consider using an irrevocable life insurance trust to own such policies.

May a grantor sell his or her retained annuity interest in a GRAT or GRUT in order to avoid inclusion of the trust corpus into his or her estate?

Yes.

Is the grantor's health a relevant consideration when creating a GRAT, GRUT or QPRT?

Yes, because a grantor who is in poor health or is terminally ill will cause the imposition of special actuarial factors in order to compute the gift tax value of the remainder interest created in a GRAT, GRUT or QPRT. *Reg. Sec. 25.7520-3(b)(3); Rev. Rul. 96-3, 1996-1 C.B. 348*. If a person has an incurable illness and if that person has a 50% or more chance that he or she will die within one year of the date of creation of the trust, then that person is considered to be "terminally ill". If such a person in fact lives beyond 18 months from the date of the creation of the trust, that person shall be presumed to be not terminally ill. These rules apply to gifts made in trust after December 13, 1995.

How does a grantor mitigate the risk of inclusion of GRAT assets in grantor's taxable estate should grantor die during the GRAT term?

As referenced above, the only scenario that assures 100% exclusion of GRAT assets from inclusion into the grantor's estate for federal estate tax purposes involves the grantor surviving the GRAT term. Should the grantor of a GRAT (or GRUT) die during the term of said trust, you can expect the IRS to take the position that the fair market value of all trust assets shall be includible in the gross estate of the grantor based upon the type of rationale and legal argument expressed in *TAM 200210009*, supra. However, there are viable counter-arguments and strategies that can be considered to address the issue of a grantor death during the trust term scenario. None of these strategies are represented as "risk-free" for IRS audit purposes because the inclusion issue remains unclear at best absent Congress implementing clarifying legislation. Short of surviving the GRAT term, the grantor/annuitant of the GRAT has the following possible planning options to choose from in order to attempt to mitigate the estate tax risk resulting from the grantor's death during the GRAT term:

1. Grantor may sell his or her retained interest, i.e., the GRAT annuity including any contingent reversionary interest to grantor's spouse or other person. *CAVEAT*: The sale might generate income tax consequences and effect of Sec. 2702 is unknown. The IRS may argue that such a sale disqualifies the GRAT.

2. Grantor may gift away his or her retained interest with same *Code Sec. 2702* caveat as above. The IRS may argue that such a gift disqualifies the GRAT.

3. Grantor sells his or her contingent reversionary interest in the GRAT, presumably to the GRAT remainderman. This scenario works as follows: grantor parent creates GRAT with a contingent reversionary interest. Grantor parent agrees by contract to sell his or her contingent reversionary interest for its fair market value to his or her children. This contract requires the grantor's estate, should grantor die during the GRAT term, to pay to children an amount equal to the value of the GRAT property reverting to and included in the grantor's estate. The contractual obligation to pay this amount to the children constitutes a deductible estate debt under *Code Sec. 2053(a),* thus reducing the taxable estate by that amount and eliminating the risk of inclusion. cf. David A. Handler's and Deborah V. Dunn's article <u>Guaranteed GRATs: GRATs Without Mortality Risk</u> published in Trust & Estates, December, 1999. This strategy probably makes the most amount of sense and has minimal risk if properly implemented.

4. Require the GRAT annuity payments to continue for the remainder of the fixed term to the grantor's estate as referenced previously. The IRS may argue that *Code Sec. 2036* still applies to cause 100% inclusion as per the *TAM 200210009* rationale.

What is the GRAT planning significance of the *<u>Walton</u>* case?

Before the implementation of *Code Sec. 2702*, taxpayers attempted to reduce the gift tax consequences of transferring property to lineal descendants by having the transferor retain an interest in the transferred property so that the value of the gift is lessened. Due to *Code Sec. 2702* and creation of the GRAT gift tax valuation rules, the strategy has changed to cause the retention of as valuable of an annuity as possible that was payable to the grantor of the GRAT. The so-called "zeroed-out" GRAT was the objective except for the fact that the IRS took the position that *Reg. Sec. 25.2702-3(e), Ex. 5,* prohibited the "zeroed-out" GRAT. In applying the aforesaid regulation, the IRS said that the retained annuity payable from a GRAT for a term of years must be valued for the shorter of the term or the grantor's life, which increases the value of the taxable gift and lowers the value of the GRAT annuity. The U.S. Tax Court held that the above regulation was invalid, thus destroying the IRS argument against a "zeroed-out" GRAT in the _Walton_ case, supra.

In _Walton_, the grantor/taxpayer created two GRATs with a two year term each and each GRAT was funded with 3,611,739 shares of Wal-Mart stock worth $100,000,024. Because the value of the stock transferred to the GRATs dropped in value, the GRAT annuity payments of $98,570,026, cumulatively, totally dissipated the principal of both GRATs leaving the GRAT remaindermen nothing at the end of the two year term. The GRATs then returned the Wal-Mart stock to the grantor. The GRATs had included language that stated that if the grantor died during the trust term that the remaining annuity payments would be paid to the grantor's estate. The IRS said this "retained contingent interest" by the grantor was not a qualified interest under *Code Sec. 2702* and applied *Reg. 25.2702-3(e), Ex. 5*, and asserted the position that a $3,821,522 gift was made. The grantor said that the contingent interest was part of the grantor's retained annuity, therefore such an interest was a "qualified interest". The Tax Court held that a fixed-term annuity payable to the grantor or the grantor's estate constituted a "qualified interest" under *Code Sec. 2702* and the value thereof should be subtracted from the value of the trust property transferred in order to calculate the remainder interest gift created by the GRAT. The Tax Court further held that *Example 5 of Reg. 25.2702-3(e)* was invalid. The practical impact of this decision is that the grantor of a GRAT can structure the terms of the GRAT (or presumably a GRUT as well) so as to create a "zero" valued taxable gift without disqualifying the trust as a GRAT.

The art of structuring a "zeroed-out" GRAT lies in the creation of a retained annuity that equals the value of the property transferred, thus resulting in a "zero" taxable gift. This sets up a "no lose" situation for the grantor of the GRAT. If the grantor survives the GRAT term, all remaining GRAT assets pass to the remaindermen without transfer taxes being paid. This is a "homerun" result for the grantor and his or her heirs. If the grantor dies during the GRAT term and there is distribution of assets to his or her estate, nothing has been lost.

The _Walton_ decision arguably demonstrates that a "zeroed-out" GRAT is possible and can be structured by creating a GRAT annuity value that equals the value of the property transferred and by requiring in the GRAT instrument that the annuity must be payable to the grantor's estate for the remainder of the original GRAT term should the grantor die during the trust term.

Can a GRAT, GRUT or QPRT be a U.S. domiciled "domes - tic asset protection trust"?

Domestically created irrevocable trusts can be used as part of an asset protection planning strategy that may include domestic asset protection trusts ("DAPTs") that are authorized by specific state law. There are a variety of different non-DAPT irrevocable trusts (such as grantor retained annuity trusts ("GRATs"), grantor retained unitrusts ("GRUTs") and qualified personal residence trusts ("QPRTs"), all of which are considered "qualified interests" trust under *Code Sec. 2702*, that have a variety of tax and non-tax estate planning benefits that also may provide incidental or limited asset protection objectives. See discussion above.

In 2004, the Alaskan legislature passed additional laws that enhance the use of Alaskan DAPTs. These new laws provide protection for QPRTs, GRATs and GRUTs. For Alaskan QPRTs, GRATs and GRUTs, a creditor of the grantor of said trust cannot seize the grantor's right to use the QPRT residence or seize the grantor's retained annuity or unitrust interest in the GRAT or GRUT. An existing trust in another state can be re-domiciled to Alaska if certain conditions are met regarding situs of trust assets, the use of a qualified trustee with requisite powers and place of trust administration.

Chapter V
The Planning Advantages of Foreign Asset Protection Trusts

Why should a U.S. citizen even consider creating a foreign situs trust for asset protection purposes?

This article will review the various asset protection benefits of foreign situs trust created by U.S. citizens. Such trusts are sometimes referred to as "international trusts", "foreign trusts", "offshore asset protection trusts" or "foreign asset protection trusts" (FAPTs). Regardless of the name given, the common elements of a FAPT are as follows: a) the FAPT is created in a non-U.S. or foreign jurisdiction; b) the FAPT is subject to and governed by the laws of a non-U.S. or foreign situs country; c) the FAPT has at least one non-resident alien trustee who manages the trust assets.

The primary advantage of a FAPT is that the laws of its foreign country of origin shall govern the viability of any creditor claims against the FAPT's grantor. Typically, the FAPT's foreign situs will provide a more beneficial set of asset protection laws and other planning advantages that would not be available to the grantor in a U.S. trust.

The standard FAPT structure will include trustee powers that allow discretionary distributions of principal or income to the grantor or other designated beneficiaries. In the event of a creditor attack against FAPT assets, the FAPT will normally include provisions that permit redomiciliation of the trust situs, i.e., so-called "flee provisions", and removal and replacement of the trustee, i.e., so-called "protector provisions".

FAPTs are now becoming more popular as a planning option for U.S. citizens due to the potential liability and risks being generated by the ever increasing flood of civil litigation in the U.S. and governmental regulation.

A FAPT should never be used as a vehicle to evade U.S. taxes or perpetrate a fraud on the grantor's creditors.

Beware of promoters of any FAPT planning structure that represents that the FAPT can be used to avoid U.S. income taxes for the grantor. Generally, this is not a true representation due to the fact that the basic FAPT shall be considered a grantor trust for U.S. income tax purposes pursuant to *Internal Revenue Code ("Code") §679. Code §679* requires that all taxable income earned by the FAPT must be reported on the grantor's individual income tax return in the year earned. The FAPT structure and grantor trust income tax treatment does not allow for income tax deferral for the U.S. grantor. Therefore, a FAPT is not used to accomplish any income tax savings for the U.S. grantor.

Why is a FAPT a better asset protection entity than a domestic trust?

A domestic trust, i.e., a trust created under the laws of a state in the U.S., is obviously governed by the laws of the state of its creation and is further subject to any applicable federal law. A FAPT, however, is only subject to the laws of the foreign jurisdiction where the FAPT is domiciled. The FAPT may contain terms that are not permitted under U.S. law.

Some typical FAPT advantages over using a domestic trust are:

1. FAPTs may provide spendthrift clause protection to a grantor beneficiary.

2. FAPTs provide a grantor with the ability to control beneficial interests in the FAPT and, in essence, control trust assets without risking trust assets to a grantor's creditors.

3. FAPTs are subject to the more favorable fraudulent transfer laws of its foreign domicile which the grantor can select.

4. FAPTs can allow for emergency removal of the trust assets to another foreign jurisdiction in the event of creditor attack or emergency removal of any trustee.

5. FAPTs are subject to the more favorable secrecy laws of its foreign domicile.

6. FAPTs may move trust assets to other foreign jurisdictions and thus create bargaining leverage over grantor's creditors.

7. FAPTs may be situated in jurisdictions that do not acknowledge U.S. civil judgments or U.S. tax assessments.

8. FAPTs are situated in non-U.S. locations where pursuing litigation against the grantor becomes practically and legally difficult.

9. FAPTs can be used to protect assets of the grantor that could otherwise not be protected under U.S. law.

10. FAPTs can provide estate planning options that are not available for U.S. trusts, ex. different rule against perpetuities treatment, and avoidance of forced heirship laws of grantor's domicile.

11. FAPTs may offer prenuptial agreement alternatives and domestic relations asset protection features.

12. FAPTs offer protection against IRS enforcement of tax liens or judgments and governmental enforcement of environmental or other judgments.

13. FAPTs provide the ability to invest in foreign investments not available to U.S. trusts.

FAPTs have some relative disadvantages vis-a-vis a U.S. trust. The cost to create and administer a FAPT is usually more expensive than a domestic trust. A client may be uncomfortable with investing assets in a non-U.S. jurisdiction due to distance, political concerns, costs of administration or other economic reasons. A FAPT should only be used where the grantor has a comfort level with the concept.

What is a "domestic asset protection trust" (DAPT) and how are DAPTs functionally different than foreign asset protection trusts (FAPTs)?

For purposes of this article, a DAPT is a U.S. domiciled trust that is administered by a U.S. trustee pursuant to state law that authorizes a so-called "domestic asset protection trust" (DAPT). Presently, there are three states, Alaska, Delaware and Missouri, that have legislation in place that authorizes DAPTs in some form in those jurisdictions.

Within the U.S., it has been the legal rule that self-settled spendthrift trusts that provide discretionary distributions to the settlor (or grantor) as a beneficiary is not effective to protect the settlor against his or her creditors attacking the trust assets. However, this rule is reversed to some extent by specific legislation in the above states, e.g. *Del. Code Ann. Tit. 12 §3570 (1997); Alaska Stat. §34.40.110(b)(2)(1997);* and *Missouri Stat. §456.080.3 V.A.M.S. (1989).* Be advised that each of these states' DAPT legislation limits the extent a settlor can be a beneficiary of the DAPT in various ways. Accordingly, DAPTs are not as flexible in terms of structure when it comes to settlor control and access of DAPT assets when compared to FAPTs. DAPTs also must utilize applicable state and

U.S. federal law concerning the statute of limitations for fraudulent transfers, rule against perpetuities, creditor rights and enforcement of judgments. Furthermore, since DAPTs are a new legal concept in the U.S., it is uncertain how courts in non-DAPT states will decide conflicting state laws in determining the settlor's rights created by the DAPT. Conceivably, there are unresolved applications of certain constitutional concepts like the Full Faith and Credit Clause, the Contract Clause found in Article I, Section 10 of the U.S. Constitution and the Supremacy Clause found in Article VI, Clause 2 of the U.S. Constitution, to DAPTs.

How is a U.S. grantor taxed on taxable income earned by a FAPT?

As mentioned above, a FAPT is income tax neutral to the U.S. grantor. This means that all taxable FAPT income is taxed to the U.S. grantor. Such income is reported on the U.S. grantor's Form 1040 for the year the income is earned. A FAPT is considered a "grantor trust" for income tax reporting purposes as required by *Code §679*. There are no income tax advantages to a U.S. grantor of a FAPT. So long as a FAPT has a U.S. beneficiary or benefits a U.S. grantor, *Code § 679* will apply to cause grantor trust tax status.

How is a FAPT treated for U.S. gift and estate tax purposes?

The answer to this question depends upon whether a completed gift is effectuated by creation of the FAPT. If a grantor has lost dominion or control of the FAPT assets so as to leave the grantor no power to change disposition of trust assets then the gift is considered completed. *Treas. Reg. §25.2511-2(b)*. However, FAPTs are usually designed as a transfer which results in an incomplete gift. In a FAPT, the grantor usually reserves rights of dominion and control of trust assets so as to cause the funding of the FAPT to be considered an incomplete gift thus causing no gift tax consequence.

When the FAPT funding is considered an incomplete gift, the entire trust corpus will be included in the U.S. grantor's estate for U.S. estate tax purposes. Irrespective of the above, the IRS requires the fling of Form 709 when the FAPT is created in accordance with *Treas. Reg. §25.2511-2(j)*. All assets passed at death of the grantor via the FAPT to beneficiaries will result in such assets receiving a stepped-up basis pursuant to *Code §1014*.

When a FAPT is funded by a U.S. grantor what are the tax consequences to that grantor?

TRA '97 created *Code §684* which causes a recognition of gain to a grantor upon the transfer of appreciated assets to a foreign trust for all transfers made after August 5, 1997. *TRA '97* repealed former *Code §1491* that imposed a 35% excise tax on such transfers to a foreign trust. The good news is that *Code §684(b)* provides an exception to the above rule in that transfers by a U.S. grantor of appreciated assets to a foreign grantor trust are not subject to the above tax scheme.

Other than the initial funding of a foreign trust, *Code §684* tax rules also apply when a U.S. trust becomes a foreign trust. In such a scenario, gain is recognized when the trust changes its U.S. domicile to a foreign domicile. A deemed transfer of appreciated assets subject to *Code §684* occurs when a U.S. trust becomes a foreign trust. Presumably, the same deemed transfer of trust assets occur and taxation results as per *Code §684* when a foreign grantor trust changes into a foreign trust is not classified as a grantor trust.

What is the tax status of a FAPT?

From a tax planning standpoint, the FAPT may be classified as a "U.S. trust" for income tax, estate tax and gift tax reporting purposes. When you have a U.S. grantor, there is no income tax advantage in being classified as a "foreign trust" for tax purposes. So-called "foreign trusts" have special tax reporting requirements not required of a U.S. trust, i.e., "domestic trust".

The term "trust" is defined by *Treas. Reg.§301.7701-4(a)* as an arrangement created by will or by inter vivos declaration whereby trustees take title to property for the purpose of protecting or conserving it for the beneficiaries under the ordinary rules applied in chancery or probate courts. The term "trust" does not include a situation where associates enter into a joint enterprise for the conduct of a business for a profit.

Beware that the IRS has issued *Notice 97-24, 1997-16, I.R.B.6* in order to attack "abusive" trust structures. Therefore, you should be sure that any FAPT shall be classified as a trust as per *Treas. Reg. §301.7701-4(a)* and that all tax reporting requirements are satisfied.

The FAPT may be designed as an irrevocable inter vivos trust that can be classified as a "U.S. trust" and a "grantor trust" as per *Code §§671-679.* As such the FAPT is income tax neutral to the U.S. grantor.

For definitional purposes, a "foreign trust" is any trust that is not defined as a "domestic trust". *Code §7701(a)(31)(B).* A "domestic trust" is defined as any trust that is subject to U.S. court primary jurisdiction over the trust's administration and one or more U.S. persons control all substantial trust decisions. *Code §7701(a)(30)(E).* These two tests for determining whether a trust is domestic or foreign are referred to as the "court test" and the "control test". The FAPT must meet both tests at any time to be a U.S. person for income tax purposes. The IRS issued *Prop. Treas. Reg. §301.7701-7* in order to interpret the definitional issues of domestic v. foreign trust classification indicated above that were imposed by the *Small Business Job Protection Act of 1996, PL 104-188 ("96 Act").*

If, for whatever reason, a FAPT is classified as a "foreign trust" for federal income tax purposes, there are special IRS reporting requirements that must be complied with at the time of the trust's creation and then annually thereafter. Beware that such a foreign trust classification may result in the FAPT being subject to withholding tax on certain U.S. source income. *Code §§6048, 1441, 1446.* An advance private letter ruling on the FAPT's trust classification may be obtained. *Rev. Proc. 98-1, 1998-1 I.R.B. 7.*

A FAPT generates no income tax advantages to the U.S. grantor. The FAPT is structured as a "grantor trust" for income tax purposes and therefore all taxable income flows through to the U.S. grantor when earned by the FAPT. *Code §679(a)(5).* Beware that non-resident alien grantors who transfer property to a foreign trust and then become U.S. residents within five (5) years of the transfer will be subject to the grantor trust rules. *Code §679(a)(4).*

Beware that when a FAPT ceases to be a grantor trust and the FAPT becomes a foreign trust, gain on the excess of the fair market value of the property over its adjusted basis will be taxed. *Code §684(a).* This rule does not apply to transfers occurring before August 5, 1997. The prior 35% excise tax imposed by *Code §1491* has been repealed.

If a FAPT is classified as a "foreign trust" for tax purposes, what are the IRS tax reporting requirements?

The following forms may be required to be filed with the IRS on behalf of the FAPT by the responsible party:

Form SS-4: Application for an Employer Identification Number.

Form 1040 NR: U.S. Non-resident Alien Income Tax Return.

Form 3520: Annual Return to Report Transactions With Foreign Trusts and Receipt of Certain Foreign Gifts.

Form 3520-A: Annual Return of Foreign Trust with U.S. Beneficiaries.

Form 926: Return by a U.S. Transferor of Property to a Foreign Corporation, Foreign Estate or Trust, or Foreign Partnership.

Form 1040 - Schedule B - Part III: U.S. Individual Income Tax Return.

Form 1041: U.S. Income Tax Return for Estates and Trusts (for "domestic trust" only).

Form TD F 90-22.1: Report of Foreign Bank and Financial Accounts.

Form 5471: Information Return of U.S. Persons with Respect to Certain Foreign Corporations (only used if FAPT owns 5% or more interest in foreign corporation).

Form 4790: Report of International Transportation of Currency or Monetary Instruments.

Form 8288 and 8288-A: Foreign Trust Transfer of U.S. Real Property.

Form 8300: Report of Cash Payment over $10,000 Received in a Trade or Business.

Form 4789: Currency Transaction Report.

Form 709: U.S. Federal Gift Tax Return.

The information reporting requirements with foreign trusts are referenced in IRS *Notice 97-34, 1997-25 I.R.B. 22.* This notice provides guidance regarding the foreign trust and foreign gift reporting provisions created by the '96 Act.

What are the civil and criminal tax penalties for failure to file returns required by *Code §6048*?

Civil penalties include:

1. Initial penalty of 35% of: 1) the value of the transferred property; 2) the value of the trust assets at the close of the year that are treated as being owned by a U.S. person; or 3) the amount of distributions received by U.S. beneficiaries.

2. Additional $10,000 penalty for each 30 day period 90 days after the IRS notifies taxpayer of a failure to file. *Code §6677.*

3. Criminal penalties include fines up to $25,000 or imprisonment of up to one year. *Code §§7203, 7206, 7207.*

What factors are important in selecting the appropriate foreign situs for a FAPT?

The primary considerations in selecting a FAPT situs are as follows:

1. The FAPT situs is a "tax haven" jurisdiction, i.e., the FAPT is not subject to local income tax, etc.

2. The costs and expenses of setting up the FAPT in the foreign situs.

3. The language and communication facilities of the situs.

4. The geographic proximity to the U.S. and the ease of travel to the foreign situs.

5. The political and economic climate of the foreign situs.

6. The availability of local banking institutions, fiduciaries, legal counsel, accountants and investment advisors in foreign situs.

7. Whether the situs is a civil law or common law jurisdiction.

8. The existence of tax treaties between the U.S. and the prospective foreign situs.

9. The status of the asset protection laws of the foreign jurisdiction.

10. The general status of the foreign jurisdiction's trust laws.

For instance, local laws regarding minimum asset funding requirements for trusts, grantor residency requirements, rule of perpetuities, restrictions, confidentiality rules, foreign exchange controls, re-domiciliation possibilities, financial disclosure laws, fraudulent transfer laws, trust enforcer or protector provisions, statutes of limitation for creditors of trusts, recognition of foreign judgments or law, spendthrift protection for grantors and governmental control of trust shall affect the situs selection decision.

What recent case law has affected foreign asset protection trust planning?

There have been several cases that have been decided recently in different jurisdictions within the United States that have cast a pall and have generated questions as to how to properly use a foreign asset protection trust. There is no doubt that some promoters and their clients have illegally or unethically used foreign asset protection trusts in order to defraud existing creditors. Obviously, the true purpose of a foreign asset protection trust is only to protect the client from future potential creditors, not existing creditors. A foreign asset protection trust, as a planning strategy, is not rendered invalid due to improper, illegal or unethical use by unscrupulous promoters or clients who intend to protect the fruits of a crime or illegally avoid a creditor's claim. See above discussion in Asset Protection Planning section of this text.

Chapter VI
CRUTs as a Planning Option

You may have an interest in utilizing a charitable remainder unitrust (CRUT) in your estate planning situation.

The purpose of this section is to review the structure, advantages and disadvantages of a CRUT. It is critical that you understand the mechanics and operative effects of using a CRUT in your estate plan.

How is a CRUT structured?

A CRUT is sometimes described as a split-interest trust. The reason for this description is that a grantor conveys, as a gift, assets to a CRUT wherein non-charitable individuals are named as beneficiaries of a unitrust interest while a charitable entity is named the trust remainderman. A CRUT must meet all the requirements set forth in *Internal Revenue Code Section 664* and the regulations promulgated thereunder. The CRUT must also comply with any applicable revenue rulings and procedures. *See, Rev. Rul. 72-395 as modified by Rev. Rul. 80-123, Rev. Rul. 82-128, Rev. Proc. 89-19, Rev. Proc. 89-20, Rev. Proc. 89-21, Rev. Proc. 90-30, Rev. Proc. 90-31, Rev. Proc. 90-32, Rev. Proc. 93-3.*

A CRUT must be formed pursuant to a written instrument and must establish both a non-charitable annuity interest for the life of one or more individuals and establish a remainder interest that passes to a qualified charitable entity. A CRUT pays a non-charitable beneficiary a variable annuity based upon a fixed percentage of the annual value of the trust assets, but in no event less than 5% per annum. *Internal Revenue Code Section 664(d)(2)(A); Regs. Section 1.664-3(a)(1) and 1.664-3(a)(2).* A CRUT may receive gifts after its initial year of funding. *Regs. Sec. 1.664-3(b).* In addition, a CRUT must contain the following characteristics:

1. The CRUT must be irrevocable.

2. The trustee of the CRUT must ascertain the fair market value of trust assets each and every year.

3. The trustee of the CRUT must pay out at least once a year a specified percentage of the value of the CRUT assets to one or more designated beneficiariebut not less than 5% per annum.

4. The CRUT annuity payments must be made either for the life a designated individual beneficiary, the lives of two or more designated individual beneficiaries or for a period of up to 20 years.

5. The charitable remainderman must qualify for a deduction under *Internal Revenue Code Section 170(c)* and it should also qualify under *Internal Revenue Code Sections 2055(a) and 2522(a). Reg. Sec. 1.664-2(a)(6); Rev. Rul. 77-385; Rev. Rul. 76-307.*

6. The CRUT must specifically permit or prohibit additional contributions.

7. The grantor of the CRUT must be prohibited from self-dealing or from making taxable expenditures.

Are you a CRUT candidate?

A CRUT is not just an estate planning vehicle for the very rich. You may be a CRUT candidate if you are interested in the following beneficial CRUT features:

1. You can avoid gift or estate taxes by transferring assets to a CRUT only if the grantor and his or her spouse are the sole non-charitable annuitants.

2. A grantor of a CRUT receives a current charitable income tax deduction for the calculated gift to the charitable remainderman in the year the CRUT is funded. This income tax deduction can be used by the grantor to off-set other income.

3. If the grantor owns highly appreciated assets that are subject to income tax, the grantor may use the CRUT to sell the highly appreciated assets and avoid capital gains tax or ordinary income tax as a result of the sale.

4. If the grantor uses highly appreciated assets to fund a CRUT, by virtue of using the CRUT as a non-taxable environment to sell those assets, the grantor will have a larger amount of principal to generate a larger cash flow annuity from that principal within the CRUT.

5. A CRUT can be designed to defer income for later distribution and can be used as a substitute or as a supplement to a qualified retirement plan.

6. Since the CRUT is a tax-free environment, the grantor can sell CRUT assets without an immediate tax consequence and then properly diversify the CRUT's investment portfolio of assets.

7. A CRUT can be an asset protected environment for the benefit of the grantor/annuitant if fraudulent transfer laws were not violated at the time of the creation and funding of the CRUT.

If some of the above factors may yield significant planning benefit to you, then you are a CRUT candidate.

Who can be a beneficiary of a CRUT?

Any individual who is living at the time of creation of the CRUT can be named as a beneficiary. *Reg. Sec. 1.664-3(a)(3).* Consequently, a CRUT income beneficiary can either be the grantor, the grantor's spouse, then living children or grandchildren, or any combination of the above individuals. But there is a caveat. Before individuals are named as beneficiaries who are not the grantor or spouse of the grantor, consider the following problems:

1. If additional income beneficiaries are younger than the grantor, the charitable deduction is reduced.

2. If younger beneficiaries are named in the CRUT, the value computed actuarially of the income stream to those younger beneficiaries shall be subject to estate tax when the grantor dies.

3. CRUT assets cannot be used to pay the grantor's estate tax, therefore other estate assets must be used to pay the tax. In other words, CRUT assets cannot be used as a source of estate tax liquidity for the grantor.

Therefore, in larger estates, it is typically prudent to designate only the grantor and his or her spouse as income beneficiaries of the CRUT. The grantor's children and grandchildren are usually provided for through other arrangements such as an irrevocable life insurance trust. The irrevocable life insurance trust (ILIT) is sometimes funded with the income tax savings generated by the creation of the CRUT and the ILIT will provide a source of cash that shall be estate tax free to the lineal heirs of the grantor. The ILIT is a cost efficient way to replace the wealth transferred to the CRUT so that lineal beneficiaries do not lose anything due to the creation of the CRUT.

What are the different CRUT formats?

There are three different types of CRUT formats:

1. A basic CRUT requires that a set annuity percentage of the fair market value of trust assets as of the beginning of each year is paid out to the designated beneficiaries without any concern to the CRUT's income. Under this format, if CRUT assets shall appreciate in value in excess of the annuity payout, then the additional income is added to the principal which shall have the effect of increasing future annuity payouts. If CRUT income is less than the required annuity payout, then trust corpus will have to be distributed to make up the difference between the annuity and the income earned.

2. A second type of CRUT is the "net income trust". *Reg. Sec. 1.664-3(a)(1)(I)(b)(1).* A net income CRUT pays out to the beneficiaries in any given year the lesser of the designated annuity percentage or the trust income for the year. This CRUT format yields a greater benefit to the charity than the non-charitable beneficiaries.

3. The third type of CRUT format is the "net income with make-up trust". It is just like the net income trust described above except that any deficiency between the required annuity and the income earned by the CRUT will be distributed to CRUT beneficiaries in a year where the trust income exceeds the fixed annuity percentage. This type of trust is obviously more complex than the basic CRUT format. However, this is the type of CRUT format that is used quite a bit in retirement planning.

How is CRUT income taxed?

CRUT distributions are taxable to the beneficiaries based upon the historic income of the trust since it was created according to the following order:

1. Distributions are taxed as ordinary income to the extent that the trust current ordinary income or any ordinary income was undistributed in prior years.

2. Distributions are taxed as capital gain to the extent of the CRUT's undistributed capital gain.

3. Distributions are taxed as other current or prior year trust income.

4. Distributions are taxed as corpus. *IRS Code Sec. 664(b) and reg. sec. 1.664-1(d)(1)(I).* The above four-tiered system of taxation of distributions to income beneficiaries by a CRUT is sometimes called the "worst in - first out"

order of income distribution. It is obvious that the CRUT's investment strategy will have a major impact on the type of tax liability generated by virtue of distributions by the CRUT to the income beneficiaries.

What kind of assets are best to fund a CRUT?

As a general rule, CRUT assets should:

1. Be very marketable and liquid.

2. Be easily valued.

3. Earn no income that is considered unrelated business, taxable income (UBTI pursuant to *Code Sec. 512*).

4. Be unencumbered by any debt and generate no debt-financed income.

5. Not violate any self-dealing rules.

6. Be well diversified, pursuant to a prudent asset allocation analysis.

Therefore, securities such as publicly traded stocks, bonds, mutual funds and closely held corporate stock are good CRUT asset candidates. Cash, life insurance and real estate are also CRUT asset candidates.

The more illiquid an asset is, the less suitable that asset is for purposes of funding a CRUT. Any asset that does not generate an adequate cash flow is an unsuitable CRUT asset. Any kind of hard-to-value asset is not a suitable CRUT asset.

What is unrelated business taxable income?

Unrelated business taxable income (UBTI) is defined to be the gross income derived by an exempt organization from any unrelated trade or business regularly carried on by it, less the deductions directly connected with the carrying out of such trade or business, both computed with certain modifications. *Internal Revenue Code Sec. 512(a)(2)*. The term "trade" or "business" carries the same meaning as is determined under *Internal Revenue Code Sec. 162*. If income is generated from the sale of goods or services, then it is a trade or business. The significance of UBTI is that if a charitable remainder trust has any unrelated business taxable income in its taxable year, the trust loses its tax-exemption for that tax year and is subject to income taxes with respect to all of its income during the entire year. *Internal Revenue Code Sec. 511(b).* Therefore, it is critical that the CRUT not invest in any asset that might generate UBTI, otherwise the CRUT will lose its tax exemption for any year in which UBTI is being generated within the CRUT.

How is the charitable deduction calculated in a CRUT?

The simple answer is that there are computer programs available that compute the amount of the allowable charitable deduction in a CRUT. The actual steps in computation are as follows:

1. Determine the assumed interest rate for the CRUT which is 120% of the federal mid-term interest rate for the month of the gift or either of the two months preceding the gift. *Internal Revenue Code Sec. 7520.*

2. Apply the appropriate IRS tables in order to find the factor for the frequency of payments and the assumed interest rate of the trust.

3. Compute the adjusted payout rate by multiplying the percentage of the value to be paid each year by the factor determined in Step 2 above.

4. Apply the appropriate IRS tables and find out the high and low factors for the adjusted payout rate and the age of the beneficiary.

5. Determine by linear interpolation between the high and low factors the exact factor for computing the charitable deduction.

6. Multiply the factor determined in step 5 above by the value of the property transferred to the trust. The result is a present value of the charitable interest and the allowable charitable deduction.

As you can see from the above, it is easier to let the computer do the work for purposes of calculating the charitable deduction.

What are the limitations on the income tax deduction that the grantor can take when setting up a CRUT?

The grantor of a CRUT is subject to the usual limitations on charitable deductions that are applicable to a gift of cash or property to a charity. The CRUT must name a charitable remainderman as defined in *Internal Revenue Code Sec. 170(b)(1)(A).* The charitable deduction can never exceed 50% of the donor's adjusted gross income. And the deduction cannot exceed 30% of the adjusted gross income if the property transferred to the trust has a built-in long-term capital gain. In either event, any excess contribution can be carried over and deducted from up to five additional years. If the trust remainderman of the CRUT is not a public charity, the deduction is limited to 30% of the adjusted gross income, or to 20% of adjusted gross income if the property has a built-in, long-term capital gain.

What are the tax and information return requirements for a CRUT?

Even though a CRUT is a tax-exempt entity, there are a variety of forms that must be filed with the Internal Revenue Service by either the grantor or the trustee of the CRUT.

1. Form 8283, if the transferred property to a CRUT exceeds $500 in value, the grantor must attach a non-cash charitable contributions information return and include it with his or her income tax return for any year in which a contribution is made. If a qualified appraisal is required, the appraisal summary portion of the form (Part B) must be completed and signed by the qualified appraiser and the trustee of the CRUT.

2. When a CRUT is created, the grantor must file a Federal Gift Tax Return (Form 709) and provide a copy of the trust instrument regardless of whether any gift tax is due. The reason for this is that even though contributions to a CRUT qualify for deduction under *Internal Revenue Code Sec. 2522,* Charitable contributions are not one of the exceptions to *Internal Revenue Code Sec. 6019,* that relieves the grantor from filing the Form 709.

3. Form 5227, must be filed by the trustee of the CRUT every year by April 15th of the year following the year for which the return is required. The Form 5227 reports trust income, deductions, accumulations and distributions for the taxable year.

4. Form 1041-A is filed by the trustee in order to report the unitrust amount. A Form K-1 is prepared in conjunction with the Form 1041-A that describes the taxable character of the distributions to the beneficiaries of the CRUT as per the four-tier system of taxation that was described above.

5. If property is transferred to a CRUT that exceeds $500 in value and is sold within two years of the date of its contribution, the trustee must file Form 8282, which shall report the structure of the donation of the property and the sale of the property.

6. Should a CRUT have any unrelated business taxable income pursuant to *Code Sec. 512*, the trustee must file a Form 1041.

7. If a trustee or a disqualified person engages in any actions which constitute self-dealing, excess business holdings, invest in a so-called jeopardizing investment or violates a taxable expenditure rule, then the trustee must file a Form 4720 Excise Tax Return by April 15th of the year following the calendar year in which the violative act occurred.

Who can be the Trustee of a CRUT and what are some problem areas for a CRUT Trustee?

There are three typical choices for a CRUT trustee:

1. The grantor and/or the grantor's spouse.

2. The charitable remainderman of the CRUT.

3. A corporate trustee such as a bank or trust company.

Beginning with *Rev. Rul. 77-285*, the grantor of a CRUT was permitted to be trustee of that CRUT. However, there are certain problems and issues that a grantor must be aware of when he or she is acting as trustee of the CRUT. There are certain powers and situations that would jeopardize the tax-exempt status of a CRUT. Here are some examples: Acts of self-dealing between the grantor and the CRUT are prohibited, acts of self-dealing include the sale, exchange or lease, a loan or other credit, furnishing goods, services or use of trust property or payment of compensation, income, or use of assets by a CRUT to a disqualified person. *Internal Revenue Code Sec. 4941(d)(1).*

A "disqualified person" may be:

1. One who contributes more than $5,000 to the CRUT or more than the grantor contributed to the CRUT.

2. A trustee of a CRUT.

3. A person who has more than 20% ownership or voting control of an entity that was a substantial contributor to the CRUT.

4. A spouse or ancestor, or lineal descendant of any of the persons named above.

If a charitable trust violates the self-dealing rule, then the CRUT shall expose itself to the excise tax imposed on private foundations. *Internal Revenue Code Sec. 4947(a)(2). Internal Revenue Code Sec. 4941* imposes an initial tax of 5% of the amount involved that is imposed on the disqualified person and an additional tax of 2 1/2% is levied upon the trustee who participates in the act of self-dealing. If an act of self-dealing is not corrected within the taxable period, additional tax of 200% of the amount involved is imposed upon the disqualified person and a tax of 50% up to a limit of $10,000 is imposed upon the trustee if the trustee refuses to agree to all or part of the correction.

A trustee must avoid investing in any investment that generates unrelated business taxable income or else the trust will lose its tax-exempt status for that tax year.

A trustee who happens to be either the grantor, his or her spouse or someone who is related or subordinate to the grantor is not allowed to have the discretion to sprinkle income among the non-charitable beneficiaries of the CRUT.

Another problem that occurs when the grantor is trustee pertains to the issue of valuation of trust assets to the detriment of the charitable remainderman of the CRUT.

Another typical problem occurs where the grantor, who is also acting as trustee of the CRUT, has pre-arranged a sale of a highly appreciated asset that was used to fund the CRUT. It is critical that the trustee of a CRUT have no expressed or implied, pre-arranged contractual obligation to sell property that was used to fund the CRUT or invest the proceeds in a specific way. *Reg. Sec. 1.664-1(a)(3), Rev. Rul. 60-370.*

Another big problem occurs where encumbered property is transferred to a CRUT. Any property that generates debt financed income should be avoided in a CRUT. The transferred of debt incumbered property to a CRUT creates "acquisition indebtedness" and unrelated business taxable income. The best solution to the debt encumbrance problem is to pay-off the debt prior to transfer to the CRUT.

The transfer of an annuity contract to a CRUT can create immediate taxation of the gain inherent in the contract. The transfer of an appreciated annuity contract will result in the grantor being taxed on all of the gain in the contract while receiving a charitable deduction only to the extent of the grantor's basis in the contract.

If the value of donated property to a CRUT as reported on the grantor's tax return exceeds the true value by 50% or more, a penalty equal to 30% of the understated tax is charged against the grantor. The trustee should always obtain a qualified appraisal made by a qualified appraiser.

The transfer by the grantor of an installment note or mortgage to a CRUT results in a taxable disposition and creates a taxable gain to the grantor in the year of transfer.

How flexible is the structure of a CRUT?

The grantor of a CRUT has a great deal of flexibility in structuring the trust terms. For example, recent private letter rulings indicate that the grantor can retain the right to change the charitable beneficiary of the CRUT, replace trustees and name himself or herself as trustee, revoke through his or her will the interest of any individual beneficiary in the CRUT and prohibit the trustee to invest in certain types of investments. *Priv. Ltr. Ruls. 9252023, 9209125, 9106008, 9138024.*

Above options are in addition to the basic choices that the grantor has in creating the CRUT, to wit:

1. The grantor chooses the non-charitable beneficiaries and the charitable remainderman.

2. The grantor chooses the trustee.

3. The grantor chooses the property to be transferred to fund the trust.

4. The grantor chooses the annual annuity unitrust amount.

5. The grantor chooses the term of the trust.

6. The grantor chooses whether to receive immediate annuity distributions or defer distributions to later years.

What are the relative advantages and disadvantages of a CRUT?

The basic advantages to the grantor of a CRUT are as follows:

1. The grantor of a CRUT receives both income tax and gift tax deductions for the value of the charitable remainder interest created by the CRUT and the CRUT can avoid estate taxes.

2. A CRUT is an income tax exempt entity. Therefore, highly appreciated

property can be transferred to the CRUT and then sold without an immediate tax consequence.

3. Due to the fact that a CRUT is tax-exempt, the principal of the trust will have a tendency to grow much faster, thus yielding greater income to the CRUT income beneficiaries during the life of the trust.

4. A CRUT can invest in tax-exempt investments that result in the annuity to the non-charitable beneficiary being tax exempt as well. As was mentioned above, there is a four-tier system of taxation of CRUT income. The character of the distribution to the non-charitable beneficiary are taxed in the following order:

Ordinary income.

Capital gain income.

Tax exempt income.

Tax free return of principal.

(To the extent that the CRUT has generated current or accumulated taxable income, then the beneficiary shall receive the same pro-rata treatment of his or her distribution from the CRUT.)

5. Grantor can serve as trustee of the CRUT.

6. A CRUT can be an asset protected environment for the grantor's assets.

Here are some disadvantages of a CRUT:

1. A CRUT requires the creation of a formal trust and tax reporting formalities.

2. A grantor should not fund a CRUT with encumbered property. A CRUT should not generate debt-financed income.

3. A CRUT should not invest in anything that generates unrelated business taxable income since that will cause the CRUT to lose its tax-exempt status for that year.

4. The grantor of a CRUT creates a taxable gift of the present value of the unitrust amount provided for the benefit of a non-spousal, non charitable beneficiary. Also, the creation of non-spousal, non-charitable beneficiaries will also generate an estate tax within the grantor's estate.

5. A CRUT should not be used to conduct an active trade or business.

How did TRA '97 impact CRUTs?

Pursuant to TRA '97, annual distributions from a CRUT must be equal to at least 5% of the initial value of the trust corpus or as revalued annually, in that annual distributions cannot exceed 50% of such value. Code Section 664(d)(1)(A), (2)(A). Pursuant to TRA '97, the actuarial value of the charitable remainder in a CRUT must be at least 10% of the net fair market value of the property transferred into the trust on the date of contribution or else the trust will not qualify as a CRUT. Code Section 664(d)(1)(D), (d)(2)(D). The 10% minimum charitable gift requirement does not apply to transfers under a will executed on or before July 28, 1997, if the decedent dies before 1999 or was on that date under a mental disability that does not permit him or her to change the disposition of his or her property under the will and does not regain competency. Code Section 2055(e)(3) has been amended to permit a CRUT to be reformed in order to meet the 10% minimum charitable gift requirement or to have the trust be declared void. In addition, on April 18, 1997, the IRS proposed regulations under Code Sections 664 and 2702 that affect CRUT planning techniques that are thought to be abusive by the Internal Revenue Service. The proposed regulations affect the following: (1) the regulations limit the use of the FLIP CRUT and require existing CRUTs to be amended or reformed; (2) the regulations require that annual payments be made by the close of taxable year instead of within a reasonable time thereafter; (3) the regulations allow an alternative valuation method using an independent appraiser for CRUTs funded with unmarketable property; (4) virtually eliminate the benefits of the near zero NIMCRUT; and (5) limit the capital gain NIMCRUT to post contribution gains. The combined effect of TRA '97, and the proposed regulations act to limit "abusive" CRUTs. For instance, accelerated CRUTs are effectively now eliminated. FLIPCRUTs can be used only if the document satisfies certain requirements. Also, NIMCRUTs that have successive income beneficiary interests and those NIMCRUTs that define capital gains as income for purposes of paying income to that income beneficiary have been practically eliminated. The upshot of TRA '97 is that standard CRUTs and NIMCRUTs are still a viable planning tool subject to the above limitations but the more exotic and "abusive" CRUT formats have been eliminated as a planning option.

May a CRUT be used as a designated beneficiary of a qualified retirement plan?

Yes, but beware that there is scant legal authority as to the tax effects.

What are the expected income tax and estate tax implications of choosing a CRUT to serve as a beneficiary of a qualified retirement plan?

In *PLR 9253038*, the taxpayer set up an inter-vivos CRUT with he and his wife as the income beneficiaries for life. The remainderman of the CRUT was a college. The taxpayer wished to designate the CRUT as the beneficiary of his qualified retirement plan account. The IRS ruled that:

1. The CRUT would not be subject to income tax upon receipt of the retirement plan funds unless there was unrelated business taxable income under *Code §512.*

2. The unitrust annuity amount to be paid to the surviving spouse will retain the same characteristics of the income received by the CRUT as determined by *Reg. §1.664-1(d)(1)(i).*

3. The present value of the surviving spouse's interest will qualify for the estate tax marital deduction under *Code §2056(a).*

4. The present value of the charitable interest in the property passing from the plan to the CRUT will qualify for the estate tax charitable deduction under *Code §2055(a).*

In *PLR 9634019*, the facts varied from *PLR 9253038* in that the CRUT beneficiaries were the taxpayer's two children. In *PLR 9634019*, the IRS ruled as follows:

1. The distribution from the taxpayer's retirement plan to the CRUT will be income with respect to a decedent as per *Code §691 ("IRD").*

2. The distribution is IRD to the CRUT but there is no income tax consequence to the CRUT unless there is unrelated business taxable income ("UBTI").

3. There is no income tax consequence to the grantor of the CRUT or his wife.

4. The unitrust amount to be paid to the CRUT beneficiaries shall retain the IRD character and constitute "first tier" ordinary income to the beneficiaries as per *Code §664(b).*

5. The present value of the remainder interest in the CRUT will qualify for the estate tax charitable deduction under *Code §2055(a).*

Most recently, *PLR 199901023* was issued which applied to a situation where a taxpayer created a CRUT with his two children as income beneficiaries and a private foundation being the CRUT remainderman. The taxpayer was a participant in a qualified retirement plan as per *Code §401(a)* and designated the CRUT as the beneficiary of taxpayer's plan account. In *PLR 199901023*, the IRS held:

1. That as per *Rev. Proc. 98-3*, no ruling will be made whether a CRUT satisfies the requirements of *Code §664* where there are one or two measuring lives or whether the transfer to the CRUT qualify for a charitable deduction under *Code §2055(e)(2)(A)*.

2. That the plan proceeds distributed to the CRUT will be included in the gross income of the CRUT as IRD and will not be includible in the gross income of the grantor's estate.

3. That the CRUT has no taxable income due to receipt of plan proceeds unless there is UBTI.

4. That in computing the hypothetical estate tax (excluding IRD items), the estate must also exclude the charitable deduction resulting from the contribution of the qualified retirement plan amounts to the CRUT.

5. That IRD is "first tier" income.

6. That the deduction provided by *Code §691(c)(1)(A)* reduces the amount of IRD that the CRUT includes in its first tier ordinary income.

Remember that private letter rulings may not be used or cited as precedent to the IRS as per *Code §6110(j)*.

Hence, designating a CRUT as a beneficiary of a qualified retirement plan constitutes a viable strategy for the right person who wishes to assume the risk of negligible legal authority.

Chapter VII
Special Needs Trust Planning For Disabled Children

What is a Special Needs or Supplemental Needs Trust?

A special needs trust is sometimes referred to as a "supplemental needs trust". Typically, this kind of trust is an irrevocable trust created during the grantor's life that is designed to supplement a handicapped or disabled individual's support needs without jeopardizing or reducing that person's eligibility for private, federal or state support and by also protecting the trust assets from that person's creditors.

A special needs trust may also be created by Will or in a revocable inter vivos trust upon the death of the grantor.

In any event, a special needs trust is structured as a "discretionary" trust that gives the trustee of such a trust the complete discretion to make distributions of income and/or principal to or for the benefit of the trust's beneficiary. In such a trust, the trust assets can only be used for the "supplemental needs" of the beneficiary which avoids the disqualification of the beneficiary from receiving governmental assistance and further prevents the beneficiary's creditors from attacking trust assets. As a result, the selection of an appropriate trustee becomes critical since that trustee will be using his or her judgment in dispensing trust income or principal only for the supplemental needs of the beneficiary.

A discretionary special needs trust can be an effective and flexible vehicle to manage assets for the benefit of a disabled beneficiary without losing governmental assistance. However, a special needs trust must not be "self-settled", i.e., the trust should not be established with the assets of the disabled person, unless the trust reimburses the government at death for services furnished to the beneficiary during his or her life. A discretionary special needs trust funded with the beneficiary's assets, regardless of whether it is created by the beneficiary, the beneficiary's parent, spouse or guardian, is classified as a "Medicaid Qualifying Trust" and will protect the beneficiary only to the extent permitted under Medicaid rules.

Medicaid rules are extremely complex and are designed to limit the amount of assets that a recipient of benefits can own or earn each year benefits are paid. Current law denies Medicaid eligibility if assets were transferred less than 36 months before application is made for benefits. A 60 month "look back period" applies to payments from certain trusts as well. This area of law varies from state to state, thereby requiring the need for competent advice.

When Should a Special Needs Trust be Used?

Special needs trusts are used to create a fund to assist in the support of a disabled child or relative and to support the elderly. Special needs trusts are also used to provide support to a spendthrift beneficiary who is not capable of managing his or her assets.

In the case of a disabled child, a problem arises when the parents are considering estate planning issues and a child is receiving or will be receiving governmental benefits. The problem to be confronted involves the threat of loss of public benefits if a disabled child inherits assets from a parent. This threat to the child's future governmental assistance will arise if the parents do not properly plan their estate. It is not necessary to disinherit the disabled child. Through the proper use of a special needs trust, the disabled child's benefits can be saved while still setting aside assets for that child's supplemental needs. To be effective, a special needs trust will preclude the disabled child beneficiary from having any power to assign, encumber, manage, direct, distribute or in any way require the trustee to make distributions from the trust. The trustee shall, in his or her absolute discretion, use trust assets for the needs of the beneficiary that are not satisfied through governmental assistance. In that way, the child's eligibility for governmental assistance is not impaired.

How Should a Special Needs Trust be Structured?

The optimum structure for a special needs trust involves the following elements:

1. The trust is irrevocable and is created during grantor's life.

2. The grantor of the trust should not be the beneficiary or remainderman.

3. The trust should not be funded with the beneficiary's assets. If it is, then the remainderman must be a qualified government entity.

4. The grantor should not retain any control over the trust assets.

5. The trust should not discharge grantor's obligation to support the beneficiary.

6. The trustee should not be the grantor, grantor's spouse, the beneficiary or any other party who would jeopardize the intent or function of the trust.

7. The trust should terminate upon the beneficiary's death.

8. The trustee should have absolute and sole discretion to distribute trust assets for the supplemental needs of the beneficiary.

9. The trust should contain a spendthrift provision.

10. A statement of the grantor's intent for the trust.

11. A direction that the trustee consider other resources of the beneficiary before making distributions.

12. A direction to the trustee that his or her discretion to distribute should only be exercised if the beneficiary's eligibility for government benefits will not be jeopardized.

13. A direction to the trustee to maximize use of government programs to pay for cost of beneficiary's care.

14. A provision allowing the trustee to accumulate income.

15. A provision that devises trust assets to remainderman upon death of the beneficiary or in the event of trust disqualification.

What are the Income Tax Implications of a Special Needs Trust?

Assuming the trust is irrevocable, the trust shall pay tax on income retained and the beneficiary shall pay income tax on taxable income distributed to him or her.

Any donor who makes a gift to fund the trust makes a taxable gift subject to the donor's annual exclusion and unified credit available.

Unless there is a transfer that is subject to the three year recapture rule for gifts made in contemplation of death, the trust assets are not includable in the donor's gross estate for federal estate tax purposes.

NOTES

NOTES

NOTES

NOTES

NOTES

NOTES

NOTES

NOTES

NOTES

For Additional copies of the book

Asset Protection Handbook

(Planning Strategies for the Florida Resident)

Price $24.95 USD, $32.50 Canada

Can be ordered by groups for study sessions on
these topics with volume discounts available

Phone Book Order Department 727-586-3306
Fax Book Order to 727-585-4209

DISTRIBUTED BY

JFP PUBLISHING
P.O. BOX 10005
LARGO, FL 33773

I would like to order ____ copies at $24.95 / ($32.50 Canada) each

for a total price $_______

Send to:

Name: ____

Address: ____

City: ______________________ State: _____ Zip: __________

Phone: ______________________